From Nomads to Pilgrims

From Nomads to Pilgrims
Stories from Practicing Congregations

Edited by
Diana Butler Bass
and
Joseph Stewart-Sicking

THE
ALBAN
INSTITUTE

Herndon, Virginia
www.alban.org

The Alban Institute
2121 Cooperative Way, Suite 100
Herndon, VA 20171-3025

Cover design by Adele Robey, Phoenix Graphics.

Library of Congress Cataloging-in-Publication Data

From nomads to pilgrims : stories from practicing congregations / edited by Diana Butler Bass and Joseph Stewart-Sicking.
    p. cm.
    Includes bibliographical references.
    ISBN-13: 978-1-56699-323-4
    ISBN-10: 1-56699-323-7
    1. Parishes—United States.   I. Bass, Diana Butler, 1959-   II. Stewart-Sicking, Joseph.

BV700.F76 2006
277.3'083—dc22

                     2005035338

10   09   08   07   06   VG   1   2   3   4   5

*To the people and pastors
of the churches that participated
in the Project on Congregations of Intentional Practice.
Thank you for all you taught us—
and most especially for becoming our friends.*

Contents

CONTRIBUTORS

DIANA BUTLER BASS directed the Project on Congregations of Intentional Practice, a Lilly Endowment–funded study of mainline Protestant vitality at the Virginia Theological Seminary in Alexandria, Virginia. She is the author of *The Practicing Congregation: Imagining a New Old Church* (Alban, 2004).

SCOTT A. BENHASE is rector of St. Philip's Episcopal Church in Durham, North Carolina.

KENNETH H. CARTER, JR., is senior pastor of Providence United Methodist Church, Charlotte, North Carolina. Previously he served as pastor of Mount Tabor United Methodist Church in Winston-Salem, North Carolina. He is the author of *A Way of Life in the World: Spiritual Practices for United Methodists* (Abingdon Press, 2004).

LILLIAN DANIEL has been senior minister of First Congregational Church in Glen Ellyn, Illinois, since 2004. From 1996–2004, she was senior minister of Church of the Redeemer (UCC) in New Haven, Connecticut. She is the author of *Tell It Like It Is: Reclaiming the Practice of Testimony* (Alban, 2005).

TODD M. DONATELLI has served as dean of the Cathedral of All Souls (Episcopal) in Asheville, North Carolina, since 1997. He has written a variety of published articles.

ERIC ELNES is senior pastor of Scottsdale Congregational United Church of Christ in Scottsdale, Arizona. He is a biblical scholar, teacher, and speaker and is the author of *The Seven Deadly Sins* in the Igniting Worship series (Abingdon Press, 2004).

PAUL E. HOFFMAN is lead pastor of Phinney Ridge Lutheran Church in Seattle, Washington. He served congregations in Texas and Nebraska prior to his ministry at Phinney Ridge.

STEVE JACOBSEN is senior pastor at Goleta Presbyterian Church in Santa Barbara, California. He is the author of *Hearts to God, Hands to Work: Connecting Spirituality and Work* (Alban, 1997) and articles exploring spirituality, leadership, work, and digital technology.

GARY D. JONES is rector at St. Stephen's Church in Richmond, Virginia, and previously was rector of Church of the Holy Communion in Memphis, Tennessee.

J. MARY LUTI is the senior minister of First Church in Cambridge, Congregational, United Church of Christ, in Harvard Square (Cambridge, Massachusetts), one of the oldest continuing congregations in North America. She is the author of *Teresa of Avila's Way*, a volume in The Way of the Christian Mystics series (Liturgical Press, 1991).

TIMOTHY SHAPIRO is the president of the Indianapolis Center for Congregations, a supporting organization of the Alban Institute funded by Lilly Endowment, Inc. For fourteen years he was the pastor of Westminster Presbyterian Church in Xenia, Ohio.

N. GRAHAM STANDISH is pastor of Calvin Presbyterian Church in Zelienople, Pennsylvania. He teaches and leads workshops in the areas of spirituality and congregational leadership. His most recent book is *Becoming a Blessed Church: Forming a Church of Spiritual Purpose, Presence, and Power* (Alban, 2005).

JOSEPH STEWART-SICKING served as project associate for the Project on Congregations of Intentional Practice.

ROY TERRY is pastor of Cornerstone United Methodist Church in Naples, Florida.

PREFACE

Not long ago, I was at Trinity Church, Wall Street, one of the oldest churches in the United States, and the church that sits right on the edge of the site of the World Trade Center. Since September 2001 the congregation has seen more than two million visitors a year pass through its historic doors. The clergy and I were talking about spiritual tourists—the throngs of people who journey to the church to understand the devastating events of the terrorist attacks. They are the unmoored, nomads in a fractured world trying to make spiritual and theological sense of the changes, violence, suffering, and war that have engulfed us.

"I've got tourists galore," sighed the Reverend Dr. Jim Cooper, Trinity's senior clergyperson. "They come. They come in droves. But I don't want them to leave as tourists. I want them to become pilgrims. I want them to connect, to know that there is something more."

Although not many other churches have two million tourists a year, Trinity is not necessarily unique. In effect, Jim Cooper's words speak to all religious communities. Every church, synagogue, mosque, and temple in the United States sits among a throng of tourists—people on a journey of self-discovery. But simply being on a spiritual journey does not automatically mean that people will find meaning. Rather, as Cooper suggested, they need to "connect" and discover that journeys can become pilgrimages. Tourists can become pilgrims.

Trips and journeys are wonderful things. Every year I joyfully anticipate my family's summer vacation at the beach. That trip lasts only a week, however; and its sole purpose is to remove us from the stress of life in Washington. We are not trying to find a new way of

life. Rather, we are seeking a change of scenery that gives us a perspective on our normal lives; rest and play that strengthen us for
things back home. Being a tourist takes us outside of daily life, and
when we are at the beach, we know that we experience the place in
an entirely different way than do the year-round locals.

But what if, instead of our yearly trip, we moved in? Becoming a
pilgrim means becoming a local who adopts a new place and new identity by learning a new language and new rhythms and practices. Unlike the tourist, a pilgrim's goal is not to escape life, but to embrace it
more deeply, to be transformed wholly as a person, with new ways of
being in community and new hopes for the world. Being a tourist
means *experiencing* something new; being a pilgrim means *becoming*
someone new. Pilgrimages go somewhere—to a transformed life.

But how does this happen? How can spiritual nomads become
pilgrims?

My friend Nora Gallagher once wrote that she came to her church
as a tourist and wound up being a pilgrim. For her, becoming a pilgrim meant walking through the seasons of a congregation's life, celebrating its festivals, living through its ordinary times, and suffering
in its dark moments. Although it was initially hard to imagine settling into a community, the quirky beauty and quiet passions of the
congregation caught her imagination. She knew she could never really understand Christianity unless she lived it. As she connected to
the church, she connected to the larger Christian tradition, and she
changed. For Nora, living Christian traditions, participating in Christian practice, and walking a Christian way bridged the gap between
nomad and pilgrim.[1]

For three years my fellow researcher Joseph Stewart-Sicking and
I studied vital mainline congregations. We discovered that they pos-
sessed a surprising capacity—they invited spiritual wanderers into a
pilgrimage through the practices of faith. We met many people like
Nora Gallagher whose lives had been transformed by joining a faith
community—not by taking a membership class or signing a pledge
card—but through participating in a congregation's story, language,
actions, and rhythms. They eagerly testified to the transformation of

the self and their churches. In a very real way, they became more than members. Whether they grew up in church or not, the people we met were converts; they experienced *metanoia*, the complete change of heart promised by God to those who follow Jesus. No prepackaged program, evangelistic strategy, or slick discipleship course made this happen. Rather, they became Christians by acting like Christians in community with people on a pilgrimage of practice. And by settling in, these tourists embarked on a different kind of journey, one that became increasingly less self-directed and increasingly aimed toward God's love and shalom.[2]

The stories that follow are stories of *metanoia*, of individual and congregational change, of people on pilgrimage. The pastors who share these stories will be the first to say that their congregations are not perfect, and that they, as the leaders, are not perfect either. They often struggled and were surprised by the Spirit along with their congregations as the community changed through practice. Indeed, in their stories, they share many of their own *metanoias*.

From these pastors and the people they serve, we learned that two practices are foundational to pilgrim communities: discernment and hospitality. Having learned to listen and to welcome, congregations then embarked on the unique practices to which God called them. Each congregation we visited was distinct, with a unique personality and specific set of practices. We asked some of the pastors in our study to reflect on a particular practice that had transformed their congregation. The authors of each chapter do not know each other, and they have not visited one another's congregations. Individually, the churches appear quirky or episodic. But when you read their stories together, it becomes surprisingly easy to discern common threads of a larger story of change in mainline Protestantism. We hope you will catch a vision of something new being birthed among us—new streams of tradition, worship, authenticity, creativity, and risk-taking. From these testimonies and the testimonies of many others we met, we feel that a new style of congregation is indeed being born—a church that is a practicing congregation, an organic community of pilgrims on a way.

Sometimes people ask us to define "practices" or "practicing congregations." In the last three years, Joseph and I have learned that such words are better left undefined, that these are concepts that can be understood only within the context of story. We hope you will come to know both Christian practices and practicing congregations as you read the stories offered here, listen to their language, imaginatively enter their lives, and sense their rhythms of faith.

This book attempts to communicate a different way of being church—not sell you a renewal program, strategy, or quick fix. It is like a collection of tales told on pilgrimage, campfire tales. We invite you to join the circle and listen as your fellow pilgrims share what they have learned. Welcome to the way.

Diana Butler Bass

Notes

1. See Nora Gallagher, *Things Seen and Unseen: A Year Lived in Faith* (New York: Knopf, 1998).

2. Although we studied vital mainline Protestant churches, we met progressive evangelicals and liberal Roman Catholics who testified to a similar pattern in their congregations. Eventually we met some Jewish pilgrims who testified to the same— and whose commitment to practice has much to teach Christians. I have no doubt that some Buddhists, Hindus, and Muslims might be able to identify with the difference between being spiritual tourists and pilgrims in faith.

ACKNOWLEDGMENTS

This book is the second based on our research, The Project on Congregations of Intentional Practice, a Lilly Endowment–funded study housed at the Virginia Theological Seminary in Alexandria, Virginia. The project studied fifty vital mainline churches to discern patterns of Christian practice in renewing local congregations. The first book, *The Practicing Congregation: Imagining a New Old Church*, outlined the theory and theology guiding the project. After its publication, interested readers (and a few reviewers too) asked us for "more stories" of the congregations. To respond to these requests, we approached some of the pastors of the participating churches and enlisted them to share some stories about how a practice transformed their congregation. *From Nomads to Pilgrims* is the result.

First and foremost, our thanks go to those pastors who worked against a tight writing deadline to share these essays. We appreciate their wisdom and friendship, two gifts that we, as researchers, never anticipated receiving when we all began this journey together three years ago. In addition to the pastor-writers in this volume, our thanks go to the pastors involved in the larger project, whose congregations echo the themes that their colleagues share here. Many thanks go to the congregations for allowing their pastors and us to offer their stories to the larger world. Without them, their openness, creativity, and faithfulness, there would be no stories to tell.

Second, we thank the Alban Institute, especially Richard Bass and James Wind, who helped shape this project during a wonderful summer retreat. Our special appreciation goes to Kristy Pullen, who came to Alban as associate director of publishing when this project was already under way, adopting it as her own, and serving as editor with grace and insight. We are grateful for the resources and assistance of Alban's entire publishing department.

And, of course, none of this would be possible without the research grant from Lilly Endowment Inc. and the support of Virginia Theological Seminary, which provided us with office space. We especially thank Craig Dykstra, Chris Coble, Martha Horne, and Mary Hix.

Finally, we thank our families for their patient love and understanding while we traveled, conducted research, interpreted data, brainstormed ideas, and worked on this book. Richard Bass is not only the publishing director at Alban, but he is Diana's partner in life. Richard and eight-year-old Emma Bass are the best of friends and pilgrimage companions for a working mom, practicing Christian, and writer. And the Reverend Megan Stewart-Sicking has not only been a sometime "reporter from the field" for her husband, but she has also been a loving partner in the journey, reminding him of the joy to be found upon the pilgrim's quest.

We feel privileged to have heard the stories of these congregations, the people who have become our friends on pilgrimage. It is a great joy to share them with you. We pray that you learn as much from them as we have.

Diana Butler Bass
Joseph Stewart-Sicking
Alexandria, Virginia
All Saints Day, 2005

INTRODUCTION

Christian Practices in the Congregation: The Structure of Vitality

Joseph Stewart-Sicking
Virginia Theological Seminary
Alexandria, Virginia

When we started the practicing congregations project to explore the life of vital mainline congregations that had creatively reappropriated traditional Christian practices, we were excited about this new "old" pattern in churchgoing we were seeing, but we were not sure whether anyone else would find these churches nearly as interesting as we did. To be honest, we began by approaching these congregations as an important counterexample to academic disdain for mainline religion. We had an important story to tell, but we imagined telling it to a small audience. Then the e-mails started coming.

As we began to post information on our Web site[1] and elsewhere, our office received a constant stream of e-mails and voice mails saying, "That's what I've always wanted to do!" or "That's my church! I didn't know any others were out there!" These messages usually were followed by invitations to speak. Instead of a mere academic interest piece, we had found something that generated hope in mainline churches long beleaguered by the dominant story of "mainline decline."

Hope is a powerful thing. Thus, all of a sudden we had a new vocation thrust upon us. No longer were we mere academics; we

1

were bearers of a new story. People were excited but expectant. They wanted something to implement, something that could change their church. And so we decided to gather and share stories—stories of hope, creativity, and God's grace; stories that might spark a new understanding of church in those who read them and encourage them to see those same stories in their own midst.

Interestingly, the stories in this book have a common pattern. Among our participants there was not a common program, common training, or even common influences—becoming a practicing congregation was not the result of any package or program. Instead, we saw a common configuration, a structure of vitality emerging in parallel across the country in radically disparate settings.

In our research we saw intentional practice. Churches worked hard at developing certain disciplines and making them the core of their life together. We saw an engagement with tradition, not as the tyranny of the dead but as a living body of wisdom. We heard stories of how churches found their identity and got where they were. And we saw churches that were transformed.

As scholars we found it interesting that there were strong parallels in this pattern to the work of philosopher Alasdair MacIntyre about living an ethical life in a modern culture.[2] But while almost all the work using MacIntyre's philosophy had heretofore focused on individual growth, we now were seeing it work in congregations. As a result of our research, we have become convinced that congregational vitality has a very similar pattern to that which others have proposed for individual development in the ethical and spiritual life. This structure of vitality, seen across the country in our congregations, has four interrelated touchstones.

Practice:
Not a Product

The first touchstone is practice itself. In embracing practices such as contemplation, testimony, hospitality, and the arts, practicing congregations run counter to the current of contemporary culture. Contemporary society seems to have packaged and commodified every aspect of life, especially spirituality and religion. If we are to believe the ads, living the good life can be as simple as buying the right product to relieve our boredom, make a fashion statement, or raise our self-esteem—and rarely does anyone else need to be involved.

But the congregations we have encountered are working at things that are not easily bought, such as becoming a community, growing in intimacy with God, and welcoming strangers. The only way to acquire these things is to practice them. And the congregations are primarily interested in these practices for their own sake, not for any external benefits such as money, members, or notoriety.

While the process may not be flashy, practicing congregations work at what they do, getting better at the practices they have chosen and finding new ways in which to grow. Practice becomes a way of life. The stories we have heard do not involve any neatly packaged programs or church growth gurus—there are no shortcuts to becoming a practicing congregation. Instead, we have heard about people working together over time, learning as they go, becoming communities dedicated to a way of life that can't be purchased.

Tradition: Keeping Christian Wisdom Alive

A second important touchstone for practicing congregations is tradition. This concept can be challenging, since many see tradition as a collection of either meaningless customs or untouchable precedents. We have found, however, that traditions of practice are imaginative and fluid.[3] For practicing congregations, tradition is a vision of the good life, expressed in the wisdom of those who have gone before and kept alive by discussion and argument. This vision of tradition fits quite nicely with one theologian's succinct description: tradition is "an argument about the meaning of true discipleship."[4]

By wrestling with the insights of the Christian tradition, practicing congregations create a vision of Christian discipleship that fits their own cultural and historical locations. In short, they try to make the wisdom of the past alive today. In doing this, practicing congregations have become soul friends with great figures throughout the church's history, such as the leaders of the early church, Benedict, Luther, Calvin, Brother Lawrence, Edwards, Wesley. And as with any good friendship, there is both respect and healthy argument. For practicing congregations, tradition is alive and sparks the imagination to find ways to live out classic ideas about Christian discipleship in a contemporary setting.

Narrative:
Not All Practices Are for Everyone

The third touchstone for the practicing congregation is narrative. As theologians have increasingly noticed, the Christian life is lived through story. Our life is, as one contemporary writer puts it, "the story we find ourselves in"[5]—of who we are and how we got here. Moreover, for Christians, our story is no ordinary story—it is the story told in Scripture of the God of Jesus Christ, whose Spirit inspires the church to work for the reign of God. It is a dramatic story, and yet it takes place in the remarkably mundane and concrete settings of churchgoers' everyday lives.

When we talked to practicing congregations, they told us stories—stories of the God who still acts and has sent them, with all their unique gifts, into a specific community, place, and time. Practicing congregations engage in discernment, finding God's will for them both as communities and as individuals. This discernment allows them to find those specific practices to which they are called—the practices that provide coherence and meaning for their own unique stories. Not every church has pursued the same practice. In fact, each church has found its own practice through a deep commitment to looking at its own special gifts and reading the needs of the community in which it finds itself. These churches have found themselves in God's story, and each one has an important and irreplaceable role to play.

Moreover, practicing congregations become places where people share stories of God in their midst. Discernment and testimony become mutually reinforcing practices that lead to a sense of joy, awe, and purpose about the congregation. Storytelling becomes a tool of evangelism, leadership, and community formation as every member of the congregation is invited to become attentive to how his or her story and the congregation's story are joined with the transformative story of God's power.

Virtue:
Practices Transform Communities by God's Grace

Practice, engaging the tradition, and storytelling become a way of life for practicing congregations, and this structure becomes a framework for vitality. But, as the testimonies of many of our participants about their church's ministries have reminded us, the growth is purely God's gift. Practicing congregations are a compelling witness to God's grace and transformative power to build both communities and individuals in virtue. And with the growth of congregational virtue, those characteristics that make possible the practice of the Christian life, comes congregational vitality. By God's grace, practicing congregations can begin to get the abundant life of God in their bones, and others can't help but become excited and attracted by this spiritual vigor.

The structure of vitality described in these four touchstones is not a straightforward recipe—take a centering prayer program, add some contemporary music, make three genograms, and then put it in the fall brochure. All of those may or may not be part of any church's structure of vitality. We found a process, not a program.

As the stories in this book show, practicing congregations may look different from one another on the outside. But they all have begun paying attention to an evolving set of practices, engaging the tradition as they understand it, and finding which practices and stories allow them to fit themselves into the story of God at work.

We hope that as you become friends with some of our friends in practicing congregations, you too will begin to develop a sense of where God is calling you, of what a great and wise inheritance you have, and of those practices you already may have begun. And by God's grace, you too will begin to see the growth already in your midst.

Notes

1. MacIntyre's work in *After Virtue*, 2nd ed. (Notre Dame, IN: Univ. of Notre Dame Press, 1984), has generated a renaissance of interest in virtue and practice among ethicists and practical theologians, for example, the work of Craig Dykstra and Dorothy Bass, "A Theological Understanding of Christian Practices," in Miroslav Volf and Dorothy Bass, eds., *Practicing Theology: Beliefs and Practices in Christian Life* (Grand Rapids: Eerdmans, 2002), and that of Stanley Hauerwas, *The Hauerwas Reader*, ed. John Berkman and Michael Cartwright (Durham, NC: Duke Univ. Press, 2001).
2. The address is www.practicingcongregations.org.
3. Diana Butler Bass, *The Practicing Congregation: Imagining a New Old Church* (Herndon, VA: Alban, 2004).
3. Kathryn Tanner, *Theories of Culture: A New Agenda for Theology*, Guides to Theological Inquiry (Minneapolis: Fortress Press, 1997).
4. Brian D. McLaren, *The Story We Find Ourselves In: Further Adventures of a New Kind of Christian* (San Francisco: Jossey-Bass, 2003).

(Re)Discovering Tradition

Becoming God's Church

Roy Terry
Cornerstone United Methodist Church
Naples, Florida

Cornerstone United Methodist Church started life only nine years ago as a church plant in the suburbs north of Naples, Florida, typical Sun Belt communities where both retirees and service workers make their homes. While many new churches follow carefully prepackaged plans that reflect current trends and tastes, Cornerstone has tried to root its life in practices that transcend time and place. As Roy Terry shares in this essay, Cornerstone has thrived not by focusing on becoming a new church, but by focusing on becoming God's church, engaging in the apostolic core of practices described in Acts 2:42 and rooting these practices in worship that breaks down human-constructed barriers.

I could feel the tension gripping my heart as the district superintendent's words came out of his mouth.

"I'm hoping you will want to start a new church."

Yep, he said it. But it took me a few minutes to realize he was serious.

It was the spring of 1996, and I was only a few weeks away from graduation at Duke Divinity School. My wife and I had traveled home to the Florida Conference of the United Methodist Church to be interviewed by the conference leadership and discern how my ministry would begin.

I never planned to launch a new congregation. I never trained in seminary to launch a new congregation. I was supposed to graduate and be placed in a church that was already established. I was supposed to be the type of pastor who would break through all the "small *t*" traditions and lead an established flock back into faithful obedience. I had reservations about the "New Church Development" movement sweeping the country and sweeping the United Methodist Church. I explained all this to the district superintendent. I was Thomas, to be sure, and maybe a little Peter thrown in for good measure.

Nevertheless, a few weeks later I received my appointment: launch a new congregation in Naples, Florida.

A few weeks after that—weeks filled with turbulent prayer and earnest reflection—I found myself at the door of a completely unexpected and new adventure.

Cornerstone United Methodist Church, now nine years past that tension-filled moment with the district superintendent, may not be the image many people conjure up when they think of a United Methodist Church. It is a thriving and vibrant congregation where the Holy Spirit blows fresh winds and where new ministries are being born with each season.

So where does one begin such a Holy Spirit adventure? What are the key practices needed to form such a community? Before launching this congregation, I wanted to find some answers. I needed to ask others I trusted to speak truthfully and offer insight. It was in a letter from Dr. Stanley Hauerwas that I picked up my first nugget of wisdom. I asked Stanley to share with me the top five things he would do if he launched a new congregation. Stanley responded:

1. Begin every meeting with at least fifteen minutes of silence and prayer.
2. Never start a men's softball team—do everything together.
3. Don't start a Sunday school. Sunday is for worship.

4. Get them involved in service—head down to the soup kitchen.
5. Never say we are starting a new church. Say we are becoming God's church!

Stanley's final statement really stuck out in my mind. What does it mean to launch a new congregation or to be a part of any congregation? He was right. A "new church" is not something new. It is but a part of God's formative work that has been handed down to us throughout the ages. To be the church is always about "becoming," about participating in God's mighty acts of salvation as handed down to us from the apostles. What we are "becoming" is part of God's grand narrative. To be the people of God is to be set apart for the work of ministry and to participate in those practices that form us. We are not about the business of doing something new. We are about sharing in the mission of God, never idle, always forming and transforming. The church is not new. The church just needs to learn to breathe again—breathe in the Holy Spirit. The church must reconnect with those things that transcend time and culture. The church must practice and celebrate the "means of grace," which are gifts from God, and not be bound by human inclinations. The work is not about technology, praise bands, or marketing. The work is about reconnecting with the gifts God has already given us, and ultimately those gifts are worship. So that is where we began at Cornerstone: becoming God's church—breathing through worship.

To breathe freely one must first cast off all the things restricting the breath and embrace the things that nourish the body. Acts 2:42 is a text that gives testimony to the core of worship: "They devoted themselves to the apostles' teaching and to the fellowship, to the breaking of bread and to prayer. Everyone was filled with awe" (NIV).

It is within this text that we find what I call the "apostolic core." Here we find Peter proclaiming the gospel and many coming to faith in Jesus Christ. But Peter and the apostles do not just abandon those persons newly committed to Christ; they bring them together into an intentional community. These intentional practices, set before the new converts, will nurture and sustain them in faith. The apostles lay out for the new community those things that transcend time as gifts from God. In gathering together, the community will participate in practices that will not only form them as the church but will also define the church before the world. They are participating in God's story, and God the Father, Son, and Holy Spirit are the main focus of all they do together. Ultimately these practices of prayer, apostolic teaching, fellowship, and breaking of bread are set in worship. When the people gather, they practice. And in practice they become for the world the body of Christ.

If it is within the apostolic core that one finds the things that nourish the body of Christ, one must also look at the things that restrict the body from breathing. When the plan to launch Cornerstone was first set forth, we gathered a group of people interested in launching this new congregation. They were given a name: "The Launch Team." Even though a more creative name for the group might have been considered, "The Launch Team" seemed to say it all.

The team prayed together and focused on worship. The team studied and reflected on the apostolic core. We knew those elements were not to be debated, and we were all very passionate about being intentional with the practices that transcended time. Having established a solid foundation for worship, the team also spent a great deal of time discussing those things that restrict the breath of God. This was probably the most fun we had in our discussions together. We shared the things we did not like about the churches we had attended in the past. Everyone was careful that the discussion did not become an opportunity to badger the body of Christ but to consider why such things might have caused disunity and harm. We talked about music styles and dress codes, how the offering was collected, and what type of people are typically seen in most mainline churches. As the discussions continued, most of these issues were directly related to human agendas. It became very clear that at times within the life of the church "Jesus Christ" was left out of the equation, replaced by self-sufficiency, comfort, and a drive for "success." So if these things stifle the breath of God, what should the church look like and how do the practices inform us of who and what we should become?

"Come as you are!" was the first theme that came to mind. If Jesus Christ is the host and all are called to participate in God's story, no one should be restricted from joining in worship. At Cornerstone no one cares what type of clothes are worn to church. The congregants are not interested in how much money anyone makes. No one really cares how everyone votes. Cornerstone loves to see a wide variety of colors, races, and nationalities in worship. The more diverse the community, the closer it is to the kingdom of God.

At the beginning of every service, we clearly explain that God has invited us all to break down the walls and barriers that separate each of us from God, from each other, and even from ourselves. These walls come in many forms: pride, prejudices, envies, jealousies, economic status, and many others. If these walls are allowed to come down, the Holy Spirit will breathe! It is in humble submission that all are equipped and able to be the body of Christ. Often it is those things that are held so sacred that become a wall erected to protect the bearer from that which is feared the most. I find, more often than not, the thing that is often feared the most is the magnificent diversity of God's people and gifts.

"Come as you are!" reaches beyond dress and carries over to the very means of celebration. If God created all things and all things are given to glorify God, worship should be a celebration of all God has to offer in that particular time and place. This celebration of diversity honors God and is directly connected to those things that transcend time. God made creative people, and they have been given many means of human expression that should be celebrated. People limit themselves when they believe worship should look a certain way or that only one style of music should be considered sacred. At Cornerstone we strive for diversity in worship. From rock 'n' roll to hymns, we sing together, and we encourage worshipers to confront their prejudices through the arts, which are celebrated through the creative people God has gifted. The arts—music, painting, dance, poetry, drama, and other means of praise—are human expressions celebrating God's creation.

Several years ago I was invited to share the Cornerstone story with a group of pastors. Each of them had been selected by the conference to launch new congregations. After spending a little time sharing, one of the pastors asked, "How did you put together your praise band? Was that one of the first things you did before launching the church?" I find this question comes to the surface every time I share with new launch pastors. It seems that much of the New Church Movement literature emphasizes "contemporary music." My response is never what everyone expects.

We did not start with a praise band at Cornerstone! We focused on worship and began singing the hymns of the church. After about two or three weeks, I brought my guitar to church and led the congregation in a new song I had just learned. That day another gentleman who played guitar asked if he could share a couple of songs and sing with me. The next thing we knew, we had a bass player, drummer, keyboard player, and singers. All of these people brought their talents together for worship. What was so magnificent about this experience was that all these gifts arose out of the congregation. Nothing was forced. Rather, through worship people connected in new ways and found a desire to share what they had to offer.

Our choir director also began incorporating some black gospel songs into the service. Soloists would ask to sing songs that touched their hearts, and some wanted to bring some sacred music into the service. From the very beginning we shared with the congregation a vision of celebration. I told them I did not want my daughter to be brought up in the faith experiencing only one style of music. I wanted her to know the classic hymns and some of the newest music available. Together these will make her a richer child of faith and help all of us confront the darkness that says God is experienced only one way.

As a result, Cornerstone is a very musical place. It is this celebration of all styles of music that has become a key component for living the gospel and living out the practices that form the community of Cornerstone. If someone asks a Cornerstone attendee if the worship service is "contemporary" or "traditional," his or her response will always be, "It is worship."

With the focus of worship being on the core elements that transcend time, the richness of the service is not identified by human agendas or *t* traditions but on things that will breathe life into dry bones. In some simple yet powerful way, when the congregation is approached by different styles of dress, music, and the arts, it learns to receive all these creative expressions as a gift. The apostolic core will always be present, but the creative gifts of the congregation might actually change with the times. I joke with the congregation about how much I loathe country music, and yet when someone sings a country-style song at Cornerstone, I have to confront my prejudice and learn to celebrate the very heart of God through the individual who has been willing to share. If I can receive a country song in the name of the Lord, I might be able to confront some of my deeper, more destructive prejudices as well. I want to look into the eyes of all the children of God and see Jesus looking right back at me.

The things that are identified as anthropological in origin I have named the "small *t*" traditions. They are influenced by time and culture. Worship at Cornerstone one week may be rockin' praise music, but the next it may be monastic chants. One week suits may be in, and the next, shorts and T-shirts. When I look back at the way I dressed twenty years ago, I ask myself, "What was I thinking?" Those *t*'s change with time, but the *T*'s transcend time and culture. The *T* traditions are the root of all worship—Scripture, fellowship, Eucharist, and prayer. Everything else is simply a means of expression and sharing. Those things do have a place in worship if they build up the body of Christ, celebrate the diversity of God's people and gifts, and do not limit our worship to human agendas and comfort zones.

Breaking through such anthropological definitions is not something new but is the major emphasis in all reform within the history of the church. Within Methodist history we find John and Charles Wesley breaking down the walls of separation as they called the church to proclaim the good news in the streets. John Wesley's cry was, "The world is my parish." The Wesleys remained faithful to the apostolic core while celebrating the vast diversity of gifts and people. Charles Wesley would go as far as using tunes to songs he heard in the local pub and placing within such common cultural expressions words of grace and life in Jesus Christ. The Wesleys took very seriously the celebration of gifts and people as they participated in those things common to the culture without forsaking the *T* traditions that transcend time. Cornerstone is a community formed in the Wesleyan tradition of Methodism.

At Cornerstone we are very clear about the "apostolic core." The congregation is reminded time and time again that the Word of God is our story and that we are a people of the Word. We share that our fellowship is not about having coffee after church but about being genuinely interested in and invested in each other's lives. The eucharist is to be shared and celebrated every time we worship, and it is at the table where the grace of God is received and experienced as Jesus Christ the host. In the eucharistic meal we participate in God's divine economy, which calls us to a new relationship with all the people of the world. We cannot control the events that take place at the table, for such mysteries define us apart from ourselves. We pray at Cornerstone, and this means time is given in the service for prayer to take its shape in the congregation's life. A few years back we took a congregational survey and asked participants to name the most important elements of worship at Cornerstone. Without question the top four elements were what forms the apostolic core. "They devoted themselves to the apostles' teaching and to the fellowship, to the breaking of bread and to prayer" (Acts 2:42 NIV).

The struggle I find in the church is a battle over *t* traditions. Within many denominations today the church's idolatry is located within the titles given to each other and the worship services in which everyone participates:

"I go to the traditional service."

"I worship at the contemporary service!"

When one embraces and passes on these labels, the breath of the
Holy Spirit is limited and the creative gifts God has given to the
church are stifled. What do "traditional" and "contemporary" mean
anyway? I thought worship was not defined by human terminology
or standards but rather by God. These worship wars within many
churches today have forced us into an idolatry that subdivides the
body of Christ. In the efforts to make the church more accessible to
seekers in the world, the church has settled for accommodation rather
than faithful practice. Today many strive to market the church, label
it, and give it a particular brand. In this practice it is hoped that
people might choose our congregation based on its entertainment
value rather than the hard call to follow Jesus Christ. Churches are
more interested in bringing in "numbers" than forming people in
faith. At Cornerstone we have all the "stuff" most churches are employing today. We have an awesome multimedia presentation, loud,
lively praise music, and a "come as you are" attitude, yet we also sing
hymns, participate in the sacred liturgies of the church, and practice
the apostolic core. If the electric power goes out at Cornerstone, the
worship will still be powerful, for at the heart of all we do is participation in the things that transcend time.

Cornerstone has been in the process of "becoming" for more
than nine years now, and we are looking forward to the continual
adventure and journey. Do we get everything right all the time? No!
But we strive to be faithful and genuine in all that we do and seek to
participate in practices that form us into the body of Christ.

Those practices have led us into other areas of our Christian life
together. Out of the heart of worship arises a desire to serve in missions, evangelism, Christian formation, care and nurture, and fellowship. We have heeded Stanley Hauerwas's suggestion not to have
Sunday school but to keep the Sabbath for worship. From worship
we go forth to educate, share, and develop ministries in which others
can participate. We pray for each other and keep in touch with our
brothers and sisters who are in need. We send mission teams around
the globe, serve in soup kitchens, build Habitat for Humanity houses,

and feed the hungry on the street. We have also become very intentional about what it means to be a member of the church.

Cornerstone has developed a twenty-eight-week Christian formation class that is required for anyone who wishes to be a member of the congregation. Drawing upon resources from the early church, as well as some modern sources, we developed a curriculum called Sojourners, a call to participation in a deeper and richer faith. This call is more than standing in front of the congregation and saying, "I do," "I will." It is journeying together and teaching practices that will sustain Christian growth. Within this time of study and preparation, participants give public affirmations, enter into covenant relationships with each other, and discern the gifts they will share with the community.

Becoming God's church is all about learning to breathe again. It is breathing in the things that make for solid formation and growth found within the gifts God has given to the church. It is breathing in the practices that call us beyond the self and to humble service through the power of the Holy Spirit. To actively participate in the practices that God has graciously given, we find freedom in the Spirit to be creative and express ourselves in wonderful and diverse ways.

Paying Attention to God

Divine Coincidences

N. Graham Standish
Calvin Presbyterian Church
Zelienople, Pennsylvania

Calvin Presbyterian Church is located in Zelienople, Pennsylvania, north of Pittsburgh—a place where demographic and economic trends make it hard for churches to thrive. While many of its neighbors have turned to conservative forms of Christianity, Calvin has found a different path. As N. Graham Standish tells in this essay, the church has focused its life on the practice of discernment—paying attention to God's presence—both in the everyday life of its members and in the way the church is governed. Through this practice, Calvin has found itself at the center of a "campaign of divine coincidences" that have brought it new life and vitality.

The Session Meeting

There are certain times when one decision determines everything. This was one of those times. I was moderating a meeting of the church session (the governing board) that would determine whether Calvin Presbyterian Church would seek to follow a more spiritual course, a way grounded in prayer and discernment, or continue to follow the course most declining mainline churches have followed. I knew that if the church decided to adopt the proposal put before it, anything was possible in terms of spiritual and numerical growth. Conversely,

17

if it rejected the proposal, my tenure there would be very short. I was too invested in the ways of spiritual formation to waste my time in a church that had little interest in spiritual growth.

Like many of today's churches, Calvin Church had ranked "spiritual development" as a priority when they sought a new pastor. But that didn't necessarily mean that the whole church, or even all its leaders, shared that vision.

At the previous session meeting, my first as their pastor, I put the agenda together in the customary way for Presbyterian sessions and church boards following the typical *Robert's Rules of Order* agenda. The main new item of business was my proposal. Preparing the way for the proposal, I spoke to the session about how managerial most of the traditional Presbyterian churches had become, and how I believed this kind of secular approach had led to our decline as a denomination. I spoke about how, in too many of our churches, we had cut off the spiritual dimension and seemed not to care any longer about prayerfully seeking and serving God's will. I talked about how too many churches had substituted the will of the majority for the will of God. I then proposed that the session create a task force to see how we could make the session meetings more prayerfully grounded and intentionally open to seeking and doing God's will. After some discussion the session agreed. A task force was created, comprised of our clerk of session, a well-respected session member (who had been involved in the national Presbyterian Church), and me.

The task force read Charles Olsen's *Transforming Church Boards into Communities of Spiritual Leaders*[1] and then discussed how we could create a more spiritually open session. We came up with four suggestions. First, we would redesign the agenda so that it was structured more like a Presbyterian worship service, with the business part of the meeting being in the place of the sermon, which would be a proclamation of God's will in our midst. Second, we would begin each meeting with the sharing of prayer concerns and the study of spiritual material designed to train the elders in prayerfully seeking

God's will. Third, recognizing that this new agenda lengthened the meetings, we would limit what came to the session for discussion and action, giving more authority to committees to make decisions as long as a decision was within their mandate and budget. The session would act only on major items affecting the life of the whole church. Finally, as moderator of the session, I would invite session members to pray before voting on motions, asking them to seek God's will rather than their own, saying, "All who sense this is God's will, say, 'Yes'; all who don't, say, 'No.'" Session members would no longer vote on what they wanted but would be encouraged to prayerfully seek together what God wanted.

At the next session meeting I prepared two agendas: a typical Presbyterian, *Robert's Rules of Order* agenda and the redesigned spiritual agenda. I proposed that they decide which agenda to follow. I also suggested that if they were to follow the more spiritual agenda, that they do it for a year so that they could live with it and experience its effects over a long period.

After some deliberation, and to my delight, the session accepted the new agenda despite the few mild skeptics in their midst. This new agenda was going to be uncomfortable because it asked them to do things not asked of them before: to deviate from generations of Presbyterian parliamentary tradition and adopt an approach that was more spiritual and less businesslike. Some worried that the meetings would be too long. Others didn't think they were prepared to say what God did or didn't want. As one elder said, "It's hard for me to believe that God cares that much about what goes on in our tiny church." I responded that I thought God was not only interested, but invested in how we run our meetings, because God wants us to seek and do God's will. What God doesn't want is to be told to wait in the hall during our meetings while we seek our own will, only to be invited in at the end when we ask God to bless what we have decided.

By agreeing to follow this new agenda, the session had decided to become centered in God. It was truly making Christ the head of the church by seeking God's will rather than its own.

Preparation for a More Spiritually Awake Church

This new, prayerful approach to meetings had its seeds in my own frustrations as a child. Except for some rare moments, such as my being blessed as a child by an Episcopal priest during communion, I never felt much connection with God in the church. Most of my God encounters happened outside the church: in the woods, with friends, or in prayer. I had a passion for God but not for the church.

In seminary and afterward I was struck by the feeling that people in the church didn't care as much about God as they did about the church. They cared more about the avenues that led to God than about God. I wanted the church to be a place where I could find and experience God. Despite being a seminary graduate, I had not been given the proper tools to help others encounter Christ.

In my frustration I sought a path that would provide answers, and I found it as I studied for a doctorate in spiritual formation, studying with Adrian van Kaam, the founder of Duquesne University's Institute of Formative Spirituality and one of the great writers in the field of spirituality. Studying in this program taught me a way of seeing Christianity and Christian life that emphasized the spiritual over the theological but in a way that made the theological clearer. I found this path by reading the writings of Christian mystics, mystics like Dorotheos of Gaza, Francis of Assisi, Julian of Norwich, Meister Eckhart, Teresa of Avila, John of the Cross, George Fox, John Wesley, Hannah Whitall Smith, Thomas Kelly, Catherine Marshall, C. S. Lewis, and Henri Nouwen. I found it by being trained as a spiritual director, a discipline of helping people discern God's presence and voice in their lives. They all helped me realize that there was a way of integrating spirituality into the life of the church that was radically rooted in the ancient practices and perceptions of mystical Christianity.

The life of a church mirrors the life of its leaders. If the pastor and leaders are prayerful, the church will be too. If the pastor and leaders are passionate about experiencing God, the church will be too. In contrast, if the church's leaders treat the church like any other organization, as a functional entity providing a religious product, the church will become a functional organization delivering a dry, prepackaged religious product. I wanted to take all I had learned on this spiritual path and use it to form an alternative church that would train church leaders to pray, seek God's will, and walk in faith, a church that would reflect my own commitment to prayer and the discerning of God's will. Slowly I developed a hypothesis of church, a hypothesis that has become my guiding theory: *a church that sincerely prays and seeks God's will in everything will be blessed by God in everything and become a blessing to the world.*

Acceptance and Transformation

Once the session accepted the new prayerful and discerning agenda, we increasingly experienced God's hand in our midst through coincidences and providences. Still, this new process wasn't easy. It was very uncomfortable at first. What was most uncomfortable was asking the question before a vote, "All who sense this may be God's will, say, 'Yes.' " It was uncomfortable because it felt like we were going against generations of church tradition.

For generations the leaders of mainline churches have been asking for the will of the majority, not the will of God. Asking elders to pray about and vote on what they thought was God's will felt like a breaking of all sorts of taboos. Not all elders liked it. Some complained to me privately, saying that it didn't feel "Presbyterian" to vote on what we thought God wanted. They said that they often didn't know what God wanted. I could only respond by saying, "I have the same discomfort. I don't know what God wants either, but I'm convinced that it's better not to know what God wants after *seeking* what God wants, than not to know what God wants after *disregarding* what God wants."

The change in the church, as a result of our change in focus, was slow and subtle in some ways yet fast and dynamic in others. Throughout that first year it became obvious that the church had many physical problems that needed to be addressed. We were growing in numbers, but we didn't have enough classroom or meeting space. The sanctuary was old and needed to be repaired and upgraded. We didn't have enough storage space for a growing drama program nor for a growing youth program. This became our first challenge in prayer. Instead of seeking to address each problem individually and piecemeal, I suggested we put together a task force to make plans to upgrade the sanctuary. When the task force was formed, I spent the first meeting laying the groundwork by asking them to seek what God wanted, not what they wanted. After months of discussion, prayer, and sifting through possibilities, plans were formulated. The task force felt called to upgrade the sanctuary in a way that gave us contemporary abilities with a traditional atmosphere.

With the sanctuary renovation plan in place, and seeing how much we had to address beyond the worship space, I suggested that we embark on a three-phase capital campaign to (Phase 1) raise funds for a renovation of the sanctuary, (Phase 2) explore how we could expand the facilities to accommodate our growing education and youth programs, and (Phase 3) establish an endowment fund and do a mission project based on a 10 percent tithe of the overall project. We estimated that the campaign would need to raise $250,000. We left the expansion phase, Phase 2, undesignated so we could prayerfully seek what God was calling us to do. Leaving Phase 2 undesignated gave us time to see what God wanted—whether that meant adding onto the building, building up, or seeking an alternative.

Taking this proposal to the session was a huge test: would the session be prayerful or fearful? Calvin Church had not attempted any kind of major building project in over forty years. The session took several meetings to discuss and pray over the project and the possibilities. When it came time to vote, I emphasized that their vote was to reflect that they sensed God's will, rather than voting on what they wanted, thought I wanted, or thought others wanted. They were to put aside all of their opinions and fears and prayerfully seek what God was calling us to do.

Eventually the session voted 11 to 1 to go forward with the project. I was willing to delay presenting the issue to the congregation if that one person who voted against it felt strongly that God was against the plan. She admitted that her reservations were her own, that she didn't really know what God wanted, and that she thought the session should move forward even if she disagreed with the plan personally. We then presented the three-phase plan to the congregation. Part of the presentation would have to deal with whether or not to use a professional fund-raising service. There was a strong sentiment on the session that we could save money by self-managing a capital campaign. Again, God seemed to act providentially to help us with making that decision.

A month earlier I had bumped into a friend of mine, a United Methodist pastor named Gary Shockley. We had met several years before when we both worked on our Ph.D.s in spiritual formation. He was working for a church fund-raising company that helps churches raise funds in a prayerful, spiritual, and scriptural way. Bumping into Gary was no mere coincidence; it was providence. The Calvin Church session, if it was going to embark on a capital campaign, needed to consider the value of using an outside company to help us. The problem in too many smaller churches is that they tend to think they can save money by raising funds themselves for projects like this. This is rarely true. Most churches raise only about one-third to one-half of their potential when they embark on home-made fund-raising campaigns. I invited Gary to speak to our session about the benefits and costs of using a professional fund raiser versus doing the project on our own. I emphasized to Gary that he was helping us discern whether to use an outside consultant, not making a pitch for his company. Gary did a wonderful job of leading us to consider the options prayerfully, and in the end the session prayerfully sensed that we were being called to use a professional fund raiser. The session then interviewed representatives of three companies and in the end decided to go with Gary's company, even though our consultant would not be Gary.

I have a firm belief that when we are prayerful and faithful, when we seek God's will in prayer and act in faith, God responds by doing wonderful things in our midst. The way the pieces were fitting together in the campaign seemed to be God's response to our prayer, and more such responses were awaiting us in the future.

We presented the whole package to the congregation in December 1997, suggesting it would cost $250,000. The congregation voted unanimously, after a month of prayerful consideration, to embark on the project. Through the campaign we received pledges of $280,000.

A Campaign of Divine Coincidences

To say that the three-year campaign and project were filled with divine coincidences would be an understatement. The campaign was filled with God's presence and power. It started with the renovation of the sanctuary. Our renovation plans included improving the chancel area and the choir loft to improve the look of the church, create more room for a growing choir and music program, and build in the ability to convert the sanctuary into a theater space for our growing and dynamic drama program. We also planned to add theatrical lighting that would allow us to improve worship and drama visibility. It was estimated that the cost to do everything would be $80,000. We quickly discovered that to upgrade the lighting meant spending $40,000 to install a new electrical service, thus bringing the cost of renovations to $120,000. We didn't know how this would impact the rest of the campaign and project, but we knew that we had no choice. We also knew that we had to trust that God was taking care of everything.

After the renovations were completed, our attention turned to Phase 2 of our campaign, which entailed looking for how we might expand our facility to create more room for classes, meeting space, and a growing youth program. A task force set up to consider options, the Phase 2 Committee, consulted with an architect to help us with future planning. The architect, who had experience with helping churches grow, told us that if we continued to grow at our present rate, we either had to consider moving the church or purchase three adjoining properties next to the church. Both the committee and the session considered these options, and both sensed that we were called to stay put and buy the properties as they became available. We trusted that if it was part of God's plan, these houses would become available in due time.

Again, providence touched us. One of those houses was already for sale, and its price had recently dropped by $10,000. Because we had money on hand from a previous sale of the church manse (the Presbyterian term for a rectory or parsonage), as well as money from the capital campaign, we were able to buy the property without going into debt. This house, which we dubbed "Faith House" (to reflect that we had faith during the campaign that God would provide, and God did), was a tremendous blessing because we were able to move our youth and education programs there. In the third year of the campaign, God acted again. The second of the three houses became available, and again, with money from the campaign, we were able to buy that house without going into debt. It was decided that this house would be rented until some time in the future when we needed the property for expansion.

In the third year of the campaign, we were able to create a $50,000 endowment fund, and we also tithed the contributions to do a mission project. In the end, the total cost of everything was $330,000—well over what we had anticipated. What was amazing was that this was almost exactly the amount that we ended up raising. We had set a tone that we would spend what we sensed we were called to spend and let God take care of the rest. It was amazing to find that our income and expenses matched almost perfectly. It was another example of divine coincidence and blessing. What was even more amazing was that two years later, in 2003, the third house the architect had designated as indispensable for expansion became available, and by combining rent from the second house with rent from this house, the mortgage paid for itself. We had added three adjoining properties, had incurred minimal debt, and were able to pay for everything without expanding our general budget.

The experience of the capital campaign and the renovation/expansion projects set an experiential foundation for the church. It taught us that when we are discerning, prayerful, and believing, God responds, even if God's response comes in an unexpected manner. When we set out on a renovation and expansion project, nobody expected that it would lead to buying three houses. Nobody thought we would raise $330,000. Nobody thought we would spend $330,000. As a congregation, we realized that when we seek God's will and trust, unexpected and wonderful blessings flow.

The result of this emphasis on prayer has been that over the years, we have increasingly brought prayer into all the areas of leadership in the church. For example, we have developed a way of budgeting that is based on asking committees to pray over their needs and costs, seeking what God is calling them to do. We also ask members to steep their giving in prayer, asking God what God is calling them to give, rather than giving what they think they can afford. The result is that over the past seven years we have increased our budget almost 300 percent and have managed to end each year with a surplus. We have created a nominating process for elders and other officers that encourages the nominating committee to pray over whom they think God is calling to be an elder, and we encourage potential officers to pray over whether they sense a call to be an elder.[2]

A Growing Staff, Worship, and Program

When I came to Calvin Church, I had read almost everything I could about starting a new pastorate. The general advice of church management experts in 1996 was that the new pastor should let go of the old staff and rebuild to suit his or her vision. Meeting the staff of Calvin Church, it was quickly apparent that God had other plans. I inherited a dynamic young staff. Bruce Smith, our music director, was a jazz pianist who had been the music director at Calvin Church since 1982. Bruce had a strong faith and sense of prayer rooted in his growing up in the Christian and Missionary Alliance Church. Bruce also had just become volunteer youth director, and he brought a dynamic vision to the youth program that included teaching youth the Bible, faith, and prayer, but also treating the youth program much like a jazz musician would treat a band. Each person could be an individual and be appreciated for his or her gifts. But it was also expected that egos would be checked at the door so everyone could work together to grow spiritually in unity.

Our drama and assistant music director, Toni Schlemmer, a former Roman Catholic with a background in theater and music, was a trained soprano who had acted professionally both in the Pittsburgh area and beyond. Toni brought a strong faith and awareness of the importance of prayer, both of which were rooted in a deep appreciation of sacraments and the drama of liturgy. Toni had developed an amazing drama program in the church that put on professional-quality plays once a year, including *Godspell, Joseph and the Amazing Technicolor Dreamcoat, Jesus Christ Superstar,* and *Children of Eden* (at the time we were only the second venue in the United States to stage this play). She also brought a classical music balance to Bruce's jazz and contemporary background.

Needless to say, I neither felt called, nor was I dumb enough, to follow the prevailing 1996 wisdom of firing all old staff members in order to hire new ones. I sensed that my role as head of staff was to nurture what was already growing.

When it came to worship, all of us on the staff developed a prayerful stance that emphasized seeking and doing what God was calling us to do. We would feel free to experiment with different forms of music and liturgy but not just for the sake of experimenting. The goal would always be to seek and do what God was calling us to do to reach spiritually across the generations. We intentionally integrated different forms of music with one question in mind: does this music and liturgy lead the people *of this church* to experience God?

One of the things that Bruce, Toni, and I sensed was the need to slowly and intentionally integrate more contemporary and other forms of music into the worship. We also realized that to engage in a worship war over music was not the path. We sensed that the wiser and more caring path would be to slowly and intentionally integrate other forms of music into worship. So we informally established a four-year plan. In the first year we integrated different forms of music into the service by having the choir sing more diverse anthems (contemporary, gospel, and world music) and occasionally having the congregation sing a contemporary hymn. We also experimented with a once-a-month contemporary service, an experiment that did not go well. The older members didn't like the worship, and the younger members weren't particularly passionate about it. After four months we stopped the experiment. Even though we try to be prayerful about everything, there are times when we cannot sense God's will without experimenting. This was one of those times.

In the second year, we created our own songbook, which included contemporary songs as well as a few older hymns not in the Presbyterian hymnal. We also decided that the last hymn every Sunday would be a contemporary one from the songbook, and the first two would be traditional hymns from the hymnal. In the third year we set the first hymn as traditional, the last as contemporary, and the middle as a song or hymn that best fit with the sermon. Finally, in year four, we felt freer to integrate all sorts of differing songs into worship, with the last hymn always being contemporary and the first being traditional. In addition, beginning in 2000, Bruce Smith and I started composing and introducing to the congregation worship songs that had the theological depth of traditional hymns with the singability of contemporary songs.

A final way that we have tried to transform worship is to build in times of silent prayer and reflection in the beginning of the service and throughout the service. We have made use of Taizé-style chants to open the service and as a response to the prayer of confession. By offering communion every Sunday in our first worship service, we have emphasized the need for sacramental prayer and experience. Even the way we order our music reflects this. We call our music selection the "march through the ages." As the service progresses, it becomes progressively less traditional and more contemporary, thus mimicking the history of the Christian church. Through all of these changes, our worship attendance has slowly increased from an average of 110 worshipers in 1996 to an average of 280 today.

In addition, we have created a Wednesday evening service of centering and healing that incorporates Taizé-style chants, *lectio divina*, and healing prayer. The music played is reflective and designed for meditation. Through all of these means our focus is both to inspire and open people to God's presence in worship rather than merely to stimulate or maintain tradition.

Building a Prayer Ministry

When I came to Calvin Presbyterian Church, I set a foundation by centering my ministry in prayer and encouraged the congregation to be a church of prayer. Healing prayer was central to that ministry. Early on in my ministry career I sensed a need for churches to recover the ministry of healing that was part of the ancient church—a healing ministry based, as much as possible, on what James says in his epistle, "Are any among you sick? They should call for the elders of the church and have them pray over them, anointing them with oil in the name of the Lord. The prayer of faith will save the sick" (5:14–15 NRSV). The ancient church was grounded in preaching, teaching, and *healing*. I sensed a call to restore healing prayer to the life of the church, but at the same time I also knew that since the practice of healing prayer had been ignored by many in the Reformation and had been diminished by the medieval Roman Catholic Church to a ministry of preparing the sick for death and the afterlife, a ministry of healing prayer would be difficult to incorporate into a modern church.

I sensed the need to start slowly, so I approached the topic in two ways. During my first year at Calvin Church, I looked for every opportunity to preach on healing and healing prayer, created a small healing prayer group, and also taught several adult education classes on it. Having introduced the congregation to the idea of healing prayer, in my second year I asked and received permission from our worship committee and the session to incorporate healing prayer into a communion service twice a year. I invited a woman named Rita Klaus, who had been healed of multiple sclerosis through healing prayer, to give a talk to our church. I also emphasized healing prayer as part of my own personal ministry of pastoral care.

As an awareness of, and an emphasis on, prayer and healing prayer grew, I invited a member of Calvin Church, Kim Gignac, to start a prayer group that would meet once a week to pray for the church, the staff, the members, those in need, the world, and other concerns. This prayer group grew so that more and more members gathered together to pray on a weekly basis. At the same time, members of the church grew to accept my emphasis on healing prayer, and more members in need requested that I do healing prayer with them. I was quickly becoming overwhelmed, but I also realized that there were members of the prayer group who were adept at healing prayer. I invited them to join a healing prayer ministry in which I would train them to visit the sick who wanted healing prayer. Their visits would not be pastoral visits, but short prayer visits. The prayer ministers would train those in need to pray for healing themselves and also pray for them and anoint them with oil on the forehead, making the sign of a Celtic cross.

Soon we began offering healing prayer once a month as part of our first worship service. The whole prayer ministry quickly grew beyond my ability to supervise it, and so I sought for someone to train and supervise the prayer ministers while also overseeing the prayer groups. One of our members, Diane McCluskey, approached me saying that she felt called by God to do this ministry even though she was intimidated by it. Within three months of Diane's becoming the prayer minister, the number of healing prayer ministers doubled and the whole prayer ministry stabilized. She has since taken the prayer ministry to new levels.

Diane is a woman who holds people deeply in prayer and experiences God's healing grace on a daily basis. Through her work, we also embarked on a new ministry, which is to have healing prayer ministers, wearing white stoles, available after each worship service to offer healing and blessing prayers to anyone in need. Diane also started a prayer shawl ministry that creates prayer shawls for those who are sick, incapacitated, and in need of prayer. Many of our members, under Diane's guidance, knit prayer shawls while praying for the eventual recipient, even if that person is unknown. To date, they have knitted more than one hundred prayer shawls.

Diane has also become an inspiration to people of other churches who have consulted with her about how to start prayer ministries in their own church. Increasingly her ministry and the whole prayer ministry plays an essential role in the life of Calvin Church.

God Wants Our Churches to Do Well

As Calvin Church moves into its one hundred sixtieth year, and as I move into my tenth year as pastor of it, much is taking place on both spiritual and practical levels. We are embarking on a $1.2 million campaign to increase office, classroom, and storage space, and we are basing this campaign on prayer. The process of determining how to accommodate our growth has been a process of discernment. We are looking for ways to consistently create small group experiences that introduce members to the writings of Christian mystics. We are seeking ways to help members integrate prayer into their everyday lives.

Certain basic beliefs have influenced me and, through me, the ministry of Calvin Church. First and foremost among them is the belief that God wants our churches to do well. This is an idea grounded in my conviction that God is constantly blessing us, and when we realize and act on that, it creates openings for these blessings.

My belief in God's presence and blessings is grounded in the writings of two of the great mystics of Christianity: Brother Lawrence of the Resurrection and Thomas Kelly. Both writers have influenced me with their belief that God can be discerned, experienced, and incarnated through prayer. The seventeenth-century mystic Brother Lawrence, in his collected writings, has said, "We do not have to be constantly in church to be with God. We can make our heart a prayer room into which we can retire from time to time to converse with Him gently, humbly and lovingly. Everyone is capable of these familiar conversations with God—some more, some less."[3] From Brother Lawrence I discovered that prayer doesn't have to be formal, but can be an ongoing conversation with God. Engaging a congregation in this ongoing conversation can create the context in which people constantly experience God, naturally and informally.

From the twentieth-century Quaker Thomas Kelly, I learned that God's Spirit and life permeate the life and ministry of the church, but we have to allow that to happen. As Kelly says:

> Deep within us all there is an amazing inner sanctuary of the soul, a holy place, a Divine Center, a speaking Voice, to which we may continuously return. Eternity is at our hearts, pressing upon our time-torn lives, warming us with intimations of an astounding destiny, calling us home unto itself. Yielding to these persuasions, gladly committing ourselves in body and soul, utterly and completely, to the Light Within, is the beginning of true life. It is a dynamic center, a creative Life that presses to birth within us. It is a Light Within which illumines the face of God and casts new shadows and new glories upon the face of men. It is a seed stirring to life if we do not choke it. It is the Shekinah of the soul, the Presence in the midst. Here is the Slumbering Christ, stirring to be awakened, to become the soul we clothe in earthly form and action. And He is within us all.[4]

In the midst of every church is a Slumbering Christ, ready to be awakened, ready to live in and through all the members, the community of Christ, the body of Christ. If we become open to that presence of Christ who is within, amazing things can happen. We can create a community of love, faith, hope, grace, healing, purpose, presence, power, and life. Ministry in this kind of church is not so much a matter of organization and program, but of seeking where Christ is already present and joining him in what he is already doing. It means being the body of Christ and placing Christ at the head, always seeking his will. Everything else flows from that.

Notes

1. Charles M. Olsen, *Transforming Church Boards into Communities of Spiritual Leaders* (Herndon, VA: Alban, 1995).
2. For more on these kinds of processes, see N. Graham Standish, *Becoming a Blessed Church: Forming a Church of Spiritual Purpose, Presence, and Power* (Herndon, VA: Alban, 2005).
3. Brother Lawrence, *The Practice of the Presence of God*, trans. Robert J. Edmonson (Brewster, MA: Paraclete Press, 1985), 89–90.
4. Thomas Kelly, *A Testament of Devotion* (San Francisco: Harper & Row, 1941), 29.

ENLARGING HOSPITALITY

Where Are the Children?

J. Mary Luti
First Church Congregational
Cambridge, Massachusetts

> *Founded in 1636, First Church Congregational in Cambridge, Massachusetts, is one of the oldest congregations in America, a church with deep roots and strong branches, a church that its leaders are proud of. But as senior minister J. Mary Luti shares in her essay, there was a problem—the church's leaders realized that there was no place for children in its community. As a result of renewed vision, First Church began to introduce children to the practices of worship through the arts. Engaging in these practices of formation and the arts, First Church has discovered that children's programs are not primarily about children; they are about shaping the entire community and welcoming the stranger within.*

A tree with strong roots, a thick trunk, and a lush canopy emerged in charcoal as members of the First Church community talked together in early 2003. Lori Hayes, one of the congregation's artists, was sprawled on the floor with a sheet of newsprint, drawing as she listened, listening as she drew. Who are we? How do we picture our life together? The questions were big, the conversation was lively, and the tree filled out, comment by comment.

At the time of this meeting, a visioning process had been under way in our church for several months. During that period, an imaginative

35

team of members new and old, led by moderator Carolyn Coffin and seminarian Kate Layzer, had convened the congregation often, prodding us to a new kind of openness. The team's charge was to help our community of theologically diverse, highly educated professionals, adept at analytical reasoning and accustomed to the expression of strong individual opinions, embrace a practice of communal discernment in the service of our church's renewal. The question they kept posing like a mantra was not "What do you think this church should be?" but "What is God's vision for us?"

As the process unfolded, we began joyfully rediscovering the gifts that have made our congregation strong for more than 370 years. We also began facing some not-so-lovely truths about our internal culture, characterized by some participants as elitist, self-satisfied, touchy about authority, and too critical. That was painful, but it also felt healthy to be shedding false images and old defenses. As we talked that morning, then, we were feeling grateful and proud.

At last it was time to see what we had been talking about. Lori held up the newsprint. It was all there—our Puritan origins, our covenants and traditions, our ministries and resources, our wonderful space, our love of worship, our great music and commitment to learning, our generosity, social justice action, and so much more. The room filled with affirmation: "What a great church!" After a minute or two, the hubbub died down. Then came a moment we may never forget. From the back of the room a voice called out, "Where are the children?"

Good question. We looked at the tree again. Not a word or symbol about kids on it anywhere. How could that be? Certainly not because we had no kids! After several years in which the number of wee ones had been fairly low, we were now welcoming many new young families into the church, and it seemed that every time we turned around, two or three women were great with child! The church was crawling with children! Yet here was a picture of a congregation in which children literally did not figure.

We tossed around some theories. Perhaps during the kid-drought we had lost the habit of attending to children. Perhaps over the years we had come to see ourselves mainly as a thinking person's church, a church of adults (many of whom are academics) and had tended therefore to reserve our best creative juices for grown-ups. Perhaps we didn't provide enough programming for children, or the right kind. We had a solid Sunday school, a children's choir, occasional speaking roles for kids in the morning service, and a more or less weekly children's sermon. Yet kids had not registered even a blip on our screen when we took up the question of congregational identity. We provided for our kids, but somehow in that providing, they had not become "us."

Where are the children? It was the question we knew we had to answer. And it prodded us over the next eighteen months toward a new ministry we call Children's Worship & Arts, or CW&A. The eventual emergence of CW&A was part of the larger movement of the Spirit in our visioning process. Subsequent listening sessions prompted by "the question" unearthed frustrations with particular features of our offerings for kids. As we reflected on our concerns, a new way of thinking began to take shape. We became persuaded that God invites children to be the church just as God invites grown-ups. And God invites kids to be the church now, belonging fully—not as guests in a grown-up church; not as building blocks for its future, valuable only when they reach adulthood; not as holy and very cute photo ops. But that was not the end of the revelation. We also came to see that although the presenting issue was the status of children, our disquiet was more pointedly about whether First Church itself was *whole*. We began to realize that a new focus on kids would not be just for the kids' sake, but for everybody's. We felt called to reshape our community to ensure *everyone* an honored place.

As we reoriented our hearts around these insights, the pressing question, "Where are the children?" expanded and deepened until it became an even more pressing one—"Is everybody here whom God has invited?" God was teaching us in this way, and in many other ways too numerous to relate here, about the virtue of *hospitality*. Sure enough, months later, our visioning process ended with a compelling call from the Spirit to center our common life decisively on that ancient practice. We received a new name to go with our new calling: "First Church in Cambridge: A Way of Hospitality." Children's Worship & Arts, now in its second year, is only one of several realizations stemming from ongoing efforts to respond faithfully to the gift of that vision.

It would be nice to say that we moved right from "the question" to the design and implementation of a great kids' program. The truth is, like many things in local church life, it was a journey of fits and starts. We would set out on one path with what seemed like a good idea only to get rerouted when, for example, the director of the children's choir resigned, creating an opportunity to rethink the role of the choir and freeing up funds for other initiatives. We had high hopes for leadership from a newly formed task force on children and youth, but for lots of reasons it never got much traction, and we had to look elsewhere for help. Many other divine knuckleballs fluttered around our plate on the way to CW&A, and we swatted gamely at them all.

Staff, parents, and other adults were occasionally unnerved by these vagaries. Indeed, much of the time we seemed to be making no discernible progress. What we had in abundant supply, however, was vision-driven determination that "the question" about our kids and the shape of our community should not go unanswered. That determination gave us the patience and forbearance necessary to persist in conversation with one another and with our circumstances until the time was ripe. Everything finally coalesced toward the end of the church's program year in June 2004. By the end of July, a thirty-something choir member and former cochairperson of the board of deacons, Sarah Higginbotham, had set out a vision for CW&A in an ambitious proposal to our executive council. (Sarah is now on staff as CW&A's coordinator. Her energy, creativity, and expertise in working with children and in supporting participating adults have been crucial to its success.)

What is CW&A? It is a ministry for children, aged 4 through 12, focused on worship as the source, center, and summit of life together in the church. It aims to help children acquire the habits and skills of Christian worship so that the full incorporation into the body conferred on them in baptism and reinforced by our congregational covenant to walk *together* in all the ways of the gospel, may become a visible reality. Through CW&A, we are equipping kids to know themselves as the church, especially when the whole body gathers in the weekly assembly. Our hope is always to be one community of praise on the Lord's Day, even if for the present our kids are not able to remain in the sanctuary with the older children and adults throughout the service every week. (As of this writing, the congregation worships "whole" at the morning service approximately one-third of the year. Our Sunday afternoon jazz and gospel service, which is now seven years old, has always incorporated kids, and we were often inspired and instructed by its success as we worked toward CW&A.)

How does the program work? At 10:00 each Sunday morning, children and adults first engage in learning—kids in Godly Play and adults in one of two, or sometimes three tracks of formation opportunities. At 11:00 everyone moves to the sanctuary for morning worship. CW&A begins when the children leave the service before the sermon. On communion Sundays (about eighteen per year), kids leave earlier and return to participate in the sacrament, to which all children of every age are always invited.

Once kids leave the sanctuary, participating adults meet them in the fellowship hall. Sarah (or occasionally one of the ministers) leads the whole group in worship for about fifteen minutes, using a simple order designed to help them feel at home with the elements and flow of Reformed worship, as well as to rehearse traditions peculiar to First Church. All this happens on the floor around a special cloth that the kids adorn each week with symbols of our faith (light, Word, cross) and with objects relating to the story of the day. The fixed order turns the rhythms of worship into second nature over time. It also creates freedom and a comfortable atmosphere that easily accommodates song, movement, and drama.

Our kids didn't "get" CW&A worship right away. During the first few weeks, they spilled raucously into the hall, lounged under the piano, meandered into the library, and clambered over the stage. They made it through the service, but barely. Although the adults present in those early weeks were wide-eyed at Sarah's kid skills—and her stamina—they could not help wondering whether things would ever improve. Of course they did. All the kids needed were structure and loving perseverance. As Sarah said, reflecting on the first year, "It was crucial not to give up on the structure, but to teach it, week after week, until the kids came to know it, trust it, and feel comfort in it."

Today few would question the effectiveness of CW&A's worship. Parents report that their kids hum CW&A songs in the backseats of minivans and insist on using them as the family grace at meals. Worship informs the kids' daily lives, and their lives inform their worship as they share prayers spontaneously each week—thanks for fun on the playground, concern for an elderly church member, grief over a pet that died, empathy for victims of natural disaster.

Practicing the skills of worship in CW&A has had other effects too. In the sanctuary, more children and adults open pew Bibles together as Scripture is read, some share hymnals and read responses from the bulletin together, and we have seen adults encourage nonreaders to hold the books and bulletins anyway, thereby helping them grasp the shape, heft, and mechanics of worship. Parts of the service that they have practiced in CW&A really catch the kids' attention, and when they are involved in leading worship, they are better prepared, more confident, more eager.

Following this brief time of worship, the arts part of CW&A gets going. Artists and other skilled adults, called from the congregation and trained by Sarah, teach movement, crafts, fine arts, and performing arts in modules of three to six weeks. Some modules prepare for liturgical seasons and feast days. During the fall of 2005, for example, children worked with one of our architect-designers, Perry Neubauer, who creates First Church's distinctive bulletin covers, to design and produce covers for Advent, Christmas, and Epiphany. In the process of exploring ways to express these seasons of celebration visually, Perry and the kids were shaped in the Spirit according to the pattern of the church's liturgical year.

A module in November 2004 engaged some kids in creating three larger-than-life-size saint puppets. They constructed the heads and hands, painted wooden pieces for the bodies, and decorated their robes with ribbons, feathers, and sparkly materials. In subsequent weeks, kids and adults named the saints and imagined their life stories. On All Saints Day, which we celebrate with communion on the last Sunday of the liturgical year, the congregation was introduced to the holy trio—St. Helen, the preacher, who prays three times a day, "doesn't trash stuff," and helps us make friends; St. Steph, the organic vegetarian, who cares about healthy eating but knows that we all need cookies, bakes them to give away, and prays *five* times a day; and St. Baja, patron saint of bicyclists, who rides a bike or a solar jet to cut down on pollution, donates money to homeless shelters (one of the congregation's ministries is a year-round shelter for homeless men), and prays *ten* times a day! These new saints processed with the choir and ministers, danced around the chancel, and took their places with the "cloud of witnesses," as the whole community celebrated the sacrament, foretaste of the kingdom, uniting the church in heaven and the church on earth.

Other arts modules have focused on Christian practices such as prayer, hospitality, the sacraments, attending to the Word, and social justice witness. One of the most compelling modules of the first year was The Great First Church Fabric Project. Over a period of weeks, kids imagined, designed, and sewed a colorful quilt to fit our massive communion table. They became so engrossed in the project that they could not be budged even for St. Steph's cookies at coffee hour! The quality of instruction from adult quilters and fabric artists made for a stunning piece of work that the children presented to the congregation in time for Easter. Received and consecrated with great joy, the quilt now covers our table every time we celebrate the eucharist. Because our kids participate in communion, they are able regularly to make the connection between the beautiful cloth they created and the beautiful community we are together when everyone—young and old—gathers for the feast.

The kids are not alone in perceiving this connection. Recently two members of the church used the quilt to adorn the table during their wedding ceremony as a way of acknowledging their union's participation in the larger unity of the church. Indeed, CW&A enlarges and enriches our Christian fellowship in many ways. For instance, Patricia Gnazzo-Pepper worked with Elizabeth Ball to create a big angel for the center of the quilt. Until CW&A there were only a few settings in our congregational life in which the mother of a teenager and a four-year-old girl could have made such a connection. Similarly, when young Aaron Hume showed unique imagination in preparing to create his piece of the quilt, project leader Sarah Fujiwara recognized his talent, moved quickly to his side, and taught him a more complex technique.

As parent Jenny Stuart noted, "The involvement of so many different adults in the arts modules not only facilitates the children's spiritual formation, but also encourages adults to form strong relationships with kids." This program has also become a vehicle for the discernment of gifts. Adults are helped to recognize talents they may not think they possess, and people with well-recognized artistic gifts stretch to find and develop additional gifts for working with children.

Through the arts our children are apprehending and expressing the mysteries of God in ways that seep in and flow out through their senses. They are "preknowing" the faith of the church, and they are making important contributions to the worship of our community. Whether they are "clowning" the gospel lesson, creating a book of photographs as a means of prayer, learning to write the Lord's Prayer in Chinese calligraphy, or singing shape note hymns in an intergenerational choir, they are no longer adjuncts to an adult worship experience. They are worshipers with us; *together* we are learning to make worship the center of our lives.

We all sense the wonder in this unfolding transformation of our community. Our music director, Peter Sykes, is a good example. Secretly, and without prompting, he created a complex, funny round out of a straightforward little song about laughter that the children were going to sing at our "And Sarah Laughed" Sunday. In the service, as the kids finished their song, the choir suddenly took it up in Peter's arrangement—to everyone's surprise and delight—and it became the anthem that day. It was a gracious, hospitable nod to the kids' contribution, a response of reciprocity that said, "You matter! You belong! We are better together!"

We sensed wonder too at our Epiphany celebration. On the night of January 6 each year, after supper and a candlelight procession through the darkened church, we renew our baptismal vows. This year, as we sang "Come All You Thirsty to the River," a First Church composition and "signature song," a leader poured water into bowls of different sizes, held by children (also of different sizes). They carried the bowls to our huge font and poured the water in, returning throughout the hymn until the baptismal basin was full. That blessed water was then used to sprinkle the people after the renewal of vows. It was a simple thing, but it moved us that kids were the ones to provide what was needed for one of our most cherished congregational rites.

CW&A, it turns out, really is for everyone. The more we work on the boundary-setting, structural consistency, and behavioral covenants our children need so that CW&A can be truly welcoming and safe for everyone, the more we are thinking about those things for adults too. As the children learn the traditions of the church, parents and other adults, some with scant Christian formation, are learning them too. As the kids absorb the ways of grown-ups, grown-ups are challenged by the ways of children. More than ever before we are committed to whole community worship as a critical formative practice. We are developing solid practices of reciprocity, communion, and celebration that strengthen every dimension of our discipleship.

Much more could be said about the plans we are making to develop this ministry—for example, helping kids grow into the ethical dimensions of worship—but that will be another chapter, another day. For now we are simply grateful that whenever God asks us,

"Where are *my* children?" we are able to respond in growing truth, "These days, Lord, they are here, there, and everywhere at First Church in Cambridge."

Resources

People

Sarah Higginbotham, MSW
Coordinator of Children's Worship & Arts
First Church in Cambridge, Congregational, UCC
saraehig@netscape.net

Daniel A. Smith
Minister of Christian Discipleship
First Church in Cambridge, Congregational, UCC
dsmith6@firstchurchcambridge.org

J. Mary Luti
Senior Minister
First Church in Cambridge, Congregational, UCC
mluti@firstchurchcambridge.org

Books

Janet Marshall Eibner and Susan Graham Walker, *God, Kids, & Us: The Growing Edge of Ministry with Children and the People Who Care for Them.* Harrisburg, PA: Morehouse, 1996.

Bonnie J. Miller-McLemore, *Let the Children Come: Reimagining Childhood from a Christian Perspective.* San Francisco: Jossey-Bass, 2003.

Elizabeth J. Sandell, *Including Children in Worship: A Planning Guide for Congregations.* Minneapolis: Augsburg Fortress, 1991.

Karen Marie Yust, *Real Kids Real Faith: Practices for Nurturing Children's Spiritual Lives.* San Francisco: Jossey-Bass, 2004.

Organizations

Revels, Inc.
www.revels.org
Revels is a nonprofit performing arts company producing music theater, recordings, and educational materials. Revels provides unique opportunities for community celebration of different cultures using traditional materials and seasonal rituals.

Oddfellows Playhouse Youth Theater
www.oddfellows.org
The largest and most active year-round youth theater in Connecticut, the Playhouse is an independent, not-for-profit organization with an arts and social service mission. The Playhouse strives to promote the growth of young people in skills, knowledge, and self-confidence through the performing arts.

MAKING SPACE FOR THE SACRED

Practicing the Presence of God in Worship

Gary D. Jones
Church of the Holy Communion
Memphis, Tennessee

> *The Episcopal Church of the Holy Communion in Memphis, Tennessee, was a sleeping giant. Already a large and prominent church, its subdued red brick façade and white interior masked a growing spiritual appetite. As Gary Jones, the church's former rector, shares in this essay, this giant was awakened through the process of developing services of contemplative worship that incorporate silence, ritual, icons, and music. Through presenting these ancient liturgical practices in fresh ways, Holy Communion discovered a contemplative ground for its ministries and found itself called to be a sacred presence at the center of the city.*

> Deep within us all, there is an amazing inner sanctuary of the soul, a holy place, a Divine Center, a speaking Voice, to which we may continuously return. Eternity is at our hearts.
> —Thomas Kelly, *A Testament of Devotion*

When worshipers and spiritual seekers arrive for a Sunday evening service at Church of the Holy Communion in Memphis, what they encounter is a darkened, quiet worship space with flickering light from a hundred or so candles. As their eyes adjust to this softly lit space, visitors can see that this traditional church has been transformed by the presence of trees and ferns that surround a central altar, along with occasional spots of color in a simple arrangement of flowers to one side, a couple of traditional icons near votive candles, and a large ceramic bowl of holy water at the head of the center aisle. One has entered a forestlike sanctuary, an interior sacred space that is soft on the physical senses, gentle on the soul, and restful for the mind.

There is a sense of spiritual calm and stillness here that many have come to relish. Unlike most who attend our morning services, a great many of those who come to worship in the evening prefer to arrive early to rest and pray. There is no chitchat in the congregation before services, but there is a palpable sense of community. The silence preceding the evening service is broken by a delicate prelude played on "gentle" instruments, such as hammered dulcimer, flute, harp, violin, or classical guitar. The prelude functions as a gentle segue into an evensong liturgy that uses words sparingly and silence liberally. There is no sermon, only a brief personal reflection offered by laity or clergy. Poetry is frequently featured as a part of the reflection. Although the evening service is unmistakably Christian, with invocations of Jesus and the Holy Trinity featuring prominently in the liturgy, we do not recite a creed in the evening. At this service we intentionally avoid the shoals of creed and dogma in favor of exploring the deeper waters of God's transcendence and mystery.

From its inception four years ago, this evening worship has grown and evolved in ways we never imagined—in numbers (from 15 to 20 in attendance to 160 or more today), in diversity (drawing all ages, as well as an array of social and religious backgrounds), and in community (liberating music and liturgy have led to an ease of fellowship among people from all walks of life). Several people have come forward to be baptized as a result of their participation in this evening service, and we recently blessed a civil marriage in the context of our worship. It is easy for newcomers to feel at home in the gently embracing intimacy of the evening service. And as newcomers develop a sense of belonging in the evening, they frequently find it easy to feel at home in the more traditional morning services, as well. On the other hand, when the portal of entry to the parish is by way of the more formal morning services, some newcomers find that this feeling of welcome and belonging can be more elusive.

Four years ago, there was no Sunday evening worship service at Church of the Holy Communion. There had been previous attempts to create a "casual" evening service, but these services never grew and eventually dwindled to nothing. However, with an influx of new lay and clergy leadership, we decided to try again. This time, instead of simply offering a casual version of the morning services, we sought to create something distinctive and fresh.

We decided that the emphasis would not be on casual dress, strumming guitars, and loose liturgy, but on ancient liturgical practices presented in fresh ways, focusing especially on contemplative traditions. We wanted to emphasize simplicity and quiet. We wanted the ambience to be welcoming, embracing, beautiful, and conducive to prayerful meditation. We wanted the worship space and the liturgy to convey both the intimacy and the mystery of God. And we decided that two of the things people most often associate with church would not take place in our evening worship—there would be no organ music, and collection plates would not be passed in the service. All of us who planned the evening service love the pipe organ, and we certainly have nothing against monetary collections, but our hope was that fewer stereotypes in worship might reduce skepticism about "institutional religion" and create an environment that promoted freer spiritual exploration and fresh apprehensions of the Divine.

The first services were based on traditional Anglican evensong, combined with the sacrament of Holy Communion. We met in a side chapel that could seat seventy people, and we altered the rigidly arranged rows of chapel seating by angling the side chairs inward, thus creating more of a sense of intimacy and community gathering. We placed candles in the windows of the chapel and arranged varying sizes of pillar and votive candles in asymmetrical patterns around the altar. Flowers from the morning services were rearranged in a single vase in a less compact, lighter and airier style. We placed the vase asymmetrically to one side of the altar, often in front, and we placed an icon on a small table with a votive candle on the other side of the chapel, closer to the congregation. The effect was to soften an otherwise stiffly arranged space and to create an environment of intimacy, spaciousness, random beauty, and embracing warmth.

We invited one or two instrumentalists to lead each evening's music. We had a flute one night and an oboe the next. We tried a recorder duet, a hammered dulcimer, a violin and cello, a flute and harp duet, a classical guitar, and so on. The emphasis was on classical music, with some fresh arrangements of traditional hymns and meditative instrumental pieces (some simple and some ethereal) that flowed naturally into periods of silence. Over time we identified certain musicians who were clearly praying through their music, not just performing, and these musicians increasingly helped us in selecting music that set the tone we were after.

Attendance at the evening services grew steadily. We experimented with the occasional use of Taizé chants, led by a cantor, and when this struck a chord with a number of people, we arranged a special trip to the Taizé community in France. Any interested parishioners were invited to join in this overseas trip to the well-known monastic community of Taizé, and the church supplemented the cost of sending a couple of our musicians. Some of our lay leaders who helped with creating the ambience for our evening services also joined in the Taizé trip, and the group returned with fresh inspiration and new ideas for our evening worship experience.

In addition to the music and liturgy of Taizé, we discovered that certain pieces of Celtic music were striking a chord with our evening worshipers. Occasionally, American derivatives of Celtic music in the songs of Appalachia were also finding a natural place in our worship. The result was an emerging blend of classical and traditional folk music along with Taizé chants and traditional hymns. Such a mixture could be jarring, but we took great care to craft liturgical experiences that were marked by a tasteful blending of ancient and modern voices, with special attention to music and prayers that evoked a calm, spiritual attentiveness and invited worshipers to a deeper place.

The popularity of these services grew, and soon we simply outgrew the chapel space. We agonized for weeks about moving this intimate worship experience into the comparatively cavernous space of the main church. No one wanted to move into the bigger space because we feared losing the intimacy and warmth that were so integral to our evening worship. Eventually, however, we simply had to make the move, and lay leaders spent days working together to simulate the embracing environment of the chapel in the larger church. One staff member visited a retreat center in Nashville where she realized that the layering of additional candles, from the altar toward the congregation, created a sense of depth and intimacy. Additionally, the strategic placement of icons and flowers helped to invite people closer and to draw the congregation together. The result was that the larger worship space could be made to feel embracing and warm while allowing those who wanted a bit more solitude to spread out.

Coincident with our move to the larger worship space, we decided to craft a Celtic evensong and communion that would make fuller use of the Celtic music that had become so meaningful to the congregation. We borrowed prayers and liturgical forms from a variety of sources—Iona, Northumbria, and elsewhere—and we brought trees, ferns, and other plants into the church to create a forestlike effect and to provide a visual complement to the nature imagery found in so many Celtic writings. In the beginning we even incorporated the soft sound of a babbling brook by putting a fountain in the midst of some of the ferns.

The Celtic service instantly became, and remains, an extraordinary draw. People regularly commented on the soothing nature of the service, the poetic imagery in the prayers, and the gracefulness of the music. On the other hand, no one wanted to let go of the Taizé evensong and communion service, with its simple chants and beautiful obbligatos. As a result, we now offer the Taizé services on the first and third Sundays of the month and the Celtic services on the second and fourth Sundays.

The Sunday evening services at Church of the Holy Communion have become well known and much loved in the larger community of Memphis. We have a number of visitors each Sunday, many of whom are from other church backgrounds and some of whom are from other faith traditions. We are in the process of producing our third CD of music that is used at the evening services, and the first two CDs continue to sell locally and across the country by way of the Internet (www.holycommunion.org). The popularity of these services among nonchurch members has led us now to host semi-annual Celtic concerts featuring music from our worship experience to give these nonmembers a way of showing their financial support. We do not sell tickets to the concerts but simply provide envelopes for special contributions anyone might like to make. The first of these concerts drew a full house and over $9,000 with very little publicity.

As time has gone by, one of our struggles has been to keep these evening worship experiences fresh and intentional. We now regularly review new prayers and music for these services, and some of our musicians have composed fresh arrangements of traditional hymns. Two of our musicians have composed special musical settings for the *Sanctus* and the *Agnus Dei* specifically for use in our Celtic communion liturgy.

In addition, although the liturgical roles and choreography for chalice bearers and readers have become set, we still have an agreement that all lay and clergy leaders for the evening service will gather one hour prior to the service to review our roles and to pray together. We gather in the chapel, go over the evening's liturgy, pray in silence, and conclude with intercessions for all who come to church that night, that they might know the healing power and presence of God in their lives. All worship leaders then vest and take their places in the chancel at least fifteen minutes before the service starts (there is no procession) so that they can be still, pray silently, and help to set the tone for other worshipers and visitors as they gather.

As our evening worship experience has evolved, we have periodically introduced spiritual practices and worship traditions that are new to many who come here. For example, one evening we put out twenty or so extra votive candles on a table near the altar. The worship leader that evening explained that many Christians through the years have found the lighting of a votive candle to be a help to them in their praying—it gives us something to do and provides a visual focus for our praying, and the presence of other lit votive candles reminds us that we are not alone in our praying.

Having introduced the practice of lighting votive candles in this simple way, the worship leader then said that anyone who wished to light a candle as a symbol of their own prayer was welcome to do so during our service. We expected that one or two people might be bold enough to come forward to light a candle; but we were taken aback when, during the music that followed, nearly everyone in the congregation got up from their seats to light a candle. Since then, the practice has become so meaningful to people that we have had a worshiper from the evening service donate four specially made votive stands for the church. Now, each Sunday evening following the prayers of the people, we put a notation in the bulletin that anyone who would like to light a votive candle as a symbol of his or her prayer is welcome to do so while our musicians play quiet instrumental pieces. Nearly everyone in the congregation comes forward, and when one is finished praying and lighting a candle, that person passes the lit taper to the next person in line. It is quite a sight, with all ages and conditions of people coming forward with their hearts full of special prayer concerns and treating each other with a kind of gentle reverence befitting another person of prayer.

Each time we have introduced a spiritual practice like this, we have included a brief explanation of the practice that we hope people will find inviting. Our invitation is for people to experiment with this practice if they like and adopt its use if they find it meaningful or helpful to them. For example, we recently introduced the use of holy water by placing a large ceramic bowl of holy water at the head of the central aisle, at the base of the chancel steps. The worship leader spoke briefly about some of the ways in which spiritual pilgrims have found holy water meaningful throughout the centuries, and we continue to print the following simple explanation:

Holy Water

Spiritual pilgrims through the centuries have found the healing and cleansing properties of holy water to be helpful in their journeys of faith. For Christians, holy water is a reminder of our baptism and the fact that we belong to God as beloved children forever. Many will touch holy water upon entering a church and make the sign of the cross as a reminder of *who* we are and *whose* we are.

The large bowl at the base of the chancel steps contains water that has been blessed according to ancient tradition. It is there for you to touch, if you wish, for healing, for cleansing, or simply for remembering that no matter what you have done or left undone, you are God's beloved forever.

Interestingly, we are finding that more and more people are adopting the use of holy water, often making the sign of the cross as they enter the church, as they come forward to light a votive candle, or as they come to receive communion.

The evening worship services at Church of the Holy Communion continue to grow and evolve. Many people have told us that they had stopped going to church until they discovered this service, and now they rarely miss a Sunday. One Jewish person who came to us by way of the evening service has already been baptized and confirmed, and another Jewish person was baptized recently. Many people who long ago left the denominations of their childhood have become devoted, confirmed Episcopalians after coming to us by way of the Sunday evening worship services.

We have tried to make it clear, however, that our goal is not to make as many people as possible into Episcopalians. Instead, our chief concern is to promote a greater awareness of the presence of God in our midst, to help more people discern how God is active in their lives and calling them into God's kingdom, and simply to manifest—for at least an hour—something of the gracious hospitality of the one God who loves us all and who has been made known to us in

Jesus. It is in this spirit, then, that we print the following welcome at the top of every Sunday evening worship bulletin:

> Welcome to this evening service.
>
> We are aware that many people who attend this service come from other churches and faith traditions, and we are delighted to have many who consider Church of the Holy Communion to be their *second* church home.
>
> The typical mixture of faith traditions represented at this service makes up a community we especially cherish. We are glad you are here.

Forming Faith

The WAY

Paul Hoffman
Phinney Ridge Lutheran Church
Seattle, Washington

Seattle is one of North America's most secular cities. The lure of the Cascades and Puget Sound make hiking and kayaking more popular Sunday activities than churchgoing. But Phinney Ridge Lutheran Church has found that Christianity can thrive in this environment. As Paul Hoffman describes in this essay, Phinney Ridge Lutheran has found that recovering the early church's practice of the catechumenate with its combination of patient hospitality, Christian formation, and liturgy provides contemporary spiritual seekers with a way home—and leads those already in the community to a renewed sense of the Christian way of life.

"Dad, did you know that God made those birds?" Dan, whose approach to God up until now had been academic, found himself in the presence of a new teacher. Three-year-old Ben had just started Sunday school, and God-talk was coming home. Dan started coming to church because he needed answers for Ben *and for himself* that went beyond the scholarly.

Kathryn came because she was troubled by deep spiritual longings she couldn't name. She was lonely, she had questions, and she needed healing from the sudden death of her husband several years earlier.

Somebody at work mentioned to her that Phinney Ridge Lutheran had "some kind of classes" for people who had questions. Maybe she should try it.

Marvin came because he was invited. At the beginning of Lent, the pastor sent out a letter that went something like this: "Are you a spouse of a member, but you've never been baptized?" Marv saw it as "the deal of the century." He'd always longed to be baptized and join the rest of his family at worship, but no one had ever asked quite so directly. He was ashamed and didn't know what to do with his shame. But the letter came, so he came too.

Paula came after seven years of walking past "those imposing front doors." She had known church and all it offered her as a little girl. But as an adult, well, she just didn't know. Could the church handle the baggage she was walking in with? Could she handle the baggage that the church no doubt was carrying in her direction? One day, walking through the door just seemed right. She screwed up her courage and went in.

Jill came because she wanted to get her two girls baptized. Without baptismal certificates, there was no way they would even be considered for Catholic school, and that was a dream Jill was not going to let die. They got baptized, all right. And in the process, Jill rediscovered a faith that she had walked away from shortly after college. She and her husband found it in such a deep and abiding way that he got baptized too. Ten years later, all four of the family members hold significant positions of leadership and trust within the community of faith.

Funny thing. None of these people came because they wanted to learn more about justification by faith apart from works of the law. They didn't even come seeking salvation or a personal relationship with Christ. They came seeking something that only the church, of all the institutions of modern American life, could provide them—a place of community, trust, ritual, and meaning grounded in the message of God's love for all people.

Rarely do those who come through the door as seekers know what they are looking for. The ones we know are much more apt to know what they *don't* want. They don't want guilt. They don't want to be preached at with meaningless pious platitudes. They don't want their lives to become suddenly more complicated. They don't want information. That can come later, once trust in a genuine and loving community has been established.

Life in Seattle is quite similar to life in the societies that cradled the early church. It is a pre-Christendom existence where almost everybody is "spiritual" but few are familiar with or actively practicing the classic spiritual disciplines of a specifically Christian faith: worship, Bible reading and study, prayer, and ministry in daily life.

Our congregation, like many other urban worship centers on the West Coast, was in quick decline at the beginning of the 1990s. So, at the leadership of then Senior Pastor Don Maier, the congregation decided to try a different approach: stop receiving members and try making disciples. Stop giving information and try forming folks in faith. Stop opening the front door only to see disillusioned and uninitiated folks streaming out the back door six weeks later. The congregation prayed and strategized itself into an experiment in creating an intentional community of faith. The classic spiritual disciplines mentioned above were perfect: worship, study, prayer, and ministry. And the path of mentoring people into a formational life of faith was already tried and true from the earliest centuries of the church's existence. At Phinney Ridge Lutheran we were not trying anything new. Instead, like many other congregations in the Roman Catholic tradition, and a growing number in the Protestant denominations, we began to rediscover the gifts of the adult catechumenate.

Now, almost twelve years into this experiment in faith, we are a transformed congregation. What began as a way of meeting new people and welcoming them into the life of the congregation has ended up being a way in which our entire congregation has discovered the spiritual richness of life in intentional community, committed to spiritual disciplines.

What does it look like?

In our process—which incidentally has been different every year that we have been involved with it—we begin to gather inquirers

over the summer and in the early months of fall. Like everywhere
else, people visit our congregation. They inquire about baptism for
themselves or for their children. Some have been around for years,
some for days. All of them are invited to consider a year's worth of
Sunday evening gatherings to meet with other Christians. There they
will reflect on the Scriptures, pray, and begin to be built into a community of love and support.

Pastoral visits and invitations of various sorts from laypersons
usually meet with an initial response that goes something like this:
"You want us to do what? And for how long?" It is, of course, a
countercultural notion that coming into a relationship with Christ
would be something other than what you could simply have for the
asking. After all, the Ethiopian eunuch asked Philip, "What is to
prevent me from being baptized?" While there's nothing to prevent
an instant "on-demand" baptism, our congregational process suggests that in the current culture this is neither wise nor effective.
Taking our cues from the early church's process, we have adopted the
stance that shaping faith takes time. Mentoring people into a life-
transforming experience of baptism or the affirmation of baptism
takes intentional effort and a reasonable period of time for reflection
and preparation. Otherwise, in the culture in which we minister,
baptism can become nothing more than one magic moment of con-
ferring salvation.

We believe, and so we practice, that baptism and its affirmation
are initiation into a community of faith that prefigures life in the
kingdom of God. Baptism is immersion into the ritual life of those
already practicing the life of disciples. There reflection, study, prayer,
and the community's support guide the seeker. Together we experience a change of the mind and the heart, a transformation of atti-
tudes and behaviors, a reordering of life's priorities as well as its beliefs.
Faith is understood as a relationship of trust, not simply assent to a
certain set of doctrines. This takes time. So we offer the gift of time.
The early church did that too. Often they took up to three years. We
offer the process of the catechumenate within the period of one liturgical year.

At Phinney Ridge Lutheran in Seattle, we call our process of the adult catechumenate The WAY. It resonates with the words of Christ in the Gospel of John, "*I am the way, the truth, and the life,*" and the name given to followers of Christ in the book of Acts.

Seekers, sponsors, and lay teachers gather every other Sunday evening at the church for a meal, served family style at tables of seven people. What starts in September as a group of seven to ten will often be forty or more by Easter. Following the meal, small Bible study groups are formed. Inquirers are paired with mentors, and a lay catechist leads the discussion. Our mentor/inquirer matches are typically done by the pastoral staff, taking into consideration each person's needs and gifts. The lay catechists are chosen by the pastoral staff as well, selected more for their obvious witness to the active life of discipleship than for their aplomb as a biblical or theological expert. The topics are straightforward and drawn from lectionary and life. The text—most frequently the gospel—from the morning is reread and a leading question or two are offered. Then the real formation begins. It is our experience that in this safe, open environment inquirers feel free to begin to make themselves vulnerable to the life-changing action of the Holy Spirit as it comes to them in this community of six or seven. Questions like the following are not uncommon: What do you mean, exactly, that you eat his body and drink his blood? I know that when you all pray you pray to someone. But who? And what do you say? How is all of this church stuff going to make any difference in my job as a software engineer?

We refer to these as primary questions. They get at the heart of what faith is about for someone seeking or reseeking a life with God and God's church. We try to make it clear that there are no stupid questions, that everything is on the table, that all inquiries are welcome. Conversations are rich and deep; there is usually a collective sigh of disappointment from the group when it is time to conclude small groups for the night and head to evening prayer.

Throughout this period of intensive and intentional study, the candidates are encouraged by their mentors to participate in the life of the congregation. If they are singers, they should sing with the choir. If they like children, they can help out in the nursery. If finances are their passion, they are encouraged to join the stewardship committee. All of these are further opportunities to be formed in a life of faith. We believe that they can and should take place even as early faith is budding or being rekindled. Our approach is simple: who are we to limit the location of the work of God's Holy Spirit?

This entire undertaking may sound like nothing more than an intensely personal process shared only in a small group or between a candidate and his or her sponsors. The entire congregation becomes involved as public rites punctuate the movement for each participant along the path of formation in faith.

As inquirers enter the process, they stand before the congregation in public worship and receive the sign of the cross "on their bodies and in their hearts," as the Evangelical Lutheran Church in America's rites themselves proclaim. This powerful ritual action of the catechumenate can be traced as far back in the church's history as the fourth century. It is a rite that likely originated with Ambrose of Milan.

These real rites taking place among real people enhance the faith journey of all who participate. Imagine, for example, the impact on congregational life as a sponsor makes the sign of the cross over an adult baptismal candidate and the presider exhorts, "Receive the cross on your heart, that Christ may dwell there by faith," and "Receive the cross on your shoulders, that you may bear the gentle yoke of Christ."

Dan, a candidate for adult baptism, stands with others walking in The WAY this year and receives the sign of the cross from his sponsor. In turn, he immediately passes on that sign to his eighteen-month-old son, Jonah, whom he holds in his arms. Together, they receive this foreshadowing sign of Christ's death. The fulfillment of this covenant awaits them in baptismal waters. Six months from now, at the vigil of Easter, they will be baptized—together, dad and son.

Harrison came to church at the suggestion of his oncologist. Now he stands among us and we proclaim, "Receive the cross on your hands, that Christ may be made known in your work." Harrison's hands are the hands of a fifty-year-old man with terminal cancer. They are hands already pocked with the stigmata of chemotherapy needles that bring physical healing. He comes as a seeker to find the spiritual healing that will help him walk in The WAY of faith to a new life in Christ in the face of sure, impending death.

We have come to say that the catechumenate in our congregation's life is "rich and messy." It is rich in that it opens all who are willing to participate in it the opportunity to be more fully open and vulnerable to one another and to the truth of life's deepest longings fulfilled in Christ. It is messy in that we are always dealing with real people, whose very real problems, questions, challenges, injustices, and hurts force us all to take our faith to a new level. In reflecting on his experience in The WAY, one candidate wrote this about his deepened experience of faith: "We can hear something a thousand times and think we understand it, and then one day it clicks and you understand it profoundly and can apply it to your life. In The WAY we were immersed in an atmosphere of faith, prayer, and Scripture. This immersion had the result of bringing religion out of Sunday morning and into everyday life, where connections can be made and new understandings take place."

In the Lenten season, candidates enter a time of intense preparation for baptism or its affirmation at the Easter vigil. Each Sunday they come before the congregation and receive the blessing of the congregation in prayer, a gift such as a Bible, hymnal, or beautiful copy of the Creed, and the assurance and support of those with whom they worship. These public rites further engage the candidates' lives in the life of the parish. Equally important, the rites affirm for those who have been part of congregational life for years and years the assurance that our faith matters. "Look at what these people are willing to say about their walk with Christ," one lifelong Lutheran in the congregation said. "If they [the candidates for baptism or its affirmation] are willing to come before the congregation week after week to make a public declaration of their faith and what it means to them, then certainly I should feel challenged to make my faith visible and active in the world."

Each time the candidates come forward for a rite, the congregation participates in prayers of blessing. We could not have imagined twelve years ago when this all began that "active Lutherans" would eventually—and with joy—find themselves participating in catechumenal rites by raising their hands in prayerful blessing each time a liturgy involving the candidates occurs in Sunday worship. Or that following the lead of candidates, longtime members of the Lutheran church who never would have considered participating in individual confession and forgiveness would follow the lead of seekers to find this a meaningful part of their personal piety. The catechumenate, in our experience, changes parish life.

Recently the opportunity to host a tent city of one hundred homeless persons who move about Seattle became a possibility for our congregation. The congregational conversation around such a bold move is not hard to imagine. Concerns ranged from how this would look in our upscale commercial neighborhood to the safety of the children in our daily preschool. What was amazing was the leadership of those who had, over the years, participated in The WAY. "We learned in our study of Scripture that our baptism meant standing side by side with those who are in need," one of the newly baptized said in one of our public decision-making forums. "Now it's time for us to live in the covenant of our baptism and offer the love of Christ to those among us who need it most. There is no question in my mind but that we should welcome the homeless of Tent City to live among us." This is parish transformation based on the gifts of the catechumenate.

Because the practice of the catechumenate is relational, we are rediscovering the relational nature of our faith. Sharing formation rather than information leads to a faith that is more clearly grounded in trust than it is in belief. Our community in Christ is certainly not perfect. But it does seem to have as one of its characteristics a healthy sense of trust among its members. This trust allows us both individually and collectively to more fully open our hearts to the incarnate Christ. Our strengthened relationships with one another, our willingness to embrace difficult questions of faith and life together, and our commitment to hospitably welcome strangers have all helped us to know more fully the welcome of a God who lives and acts among us.

During a recent reunion of our WAY participants from the past twelve years, one of the parish's earliest candidates said this about the incarnation of Christ through our congregation's catechumenate community: "Thank you for your welcome and your hospitality. And thank you for having the patience and faith to trust your pastors to preach, minister, model, and lead in an environment where we support and form each other in the image of Christ as a catechumenate community. It is slow, labor-intensive, messy, wonderful work. …When peace seems hopeless, or a friend dies, or a family member gets sick, your welcome and hospitality show me the power of the Word and the table and the font in all situations. Every situation. Christ in the middle offering an invitation. But I can't see Christ alone. I can't. I need help. And so through the stirrings of the Holy Spirit, Christ calls us to follow. To invite as we have been invited. To be hospitable with the warmth and lavishness of Christ and to show up to be Christ in the world and in each other's lives. You showed up for me. I've never been the same. Thank you for being the light of Christ when I didn't even know it was dark and for being the light of Christ when it has been so dark I couldn't believe there was any light. I will never be the same."

Since 1994 the adult catechumenate in our congregation has involved 362 persons as candidates, sponsors, catechists, and leadership team members. This is roughly equal to our present Sunday worship attendance. With such a high rate of involvement among the established congregation and those new to our household of faith, we have learned that the miraculous takes place. It is not *their* faith, but *ours* that has been enriched. In the end, it is not about *us* and *them*. It is about all of us being continually formed in faith. Pilgrims together, along The WAY.

From time to time we pray in public worship that "God will bring yet others to this font to receive the gifts of baptism." Each Easter vigil we are living witnesses to answered prayer. God sends us children and adults to welcome into the community. By God's grace, and in the name of Christ, crucified and risen, we are willing partners in leading them to the waters, even as Philip led the Ethiopian eunuch so many years ago. How blessed we are to be partners with the Almighty One in this holy, healing work.

Practicing Worship

From Message to Incarnation

Eric Elnes
Scottsdale Congregational United Church of Christ
Scottsdale, Arizona

Established in 1959, Scottsdale Congregational United Church of Christ in Scottsdale, Arizona, had found itself in the midst of midlife doldrums, wondering like many other middle-aged churches where new spiritual energy might come from. In this essay, pastor Eric Elnes shares the story of how a Bible study led to an unexpected renewal of worship. Through a process of risk taking and practice, the congregation found renewed vitality, culminating in a change from "message-based" to "incarnational" worship.

I can hardly wait to get to worship each Sunday morning. I'm like a little kid on Christmas morning waiting for the signal from parents to dash downstairs and open presents stacked under the tree. I keep thinking the feeling will go away, or at least wane a bit, but it doesn't. If anything, it gets more intense.

Part of my excitement stems from knowing that most of the people I'll be joining in worship feel the same way I do. We are all a bit giddy, wondering what gifts worship will bring us. The other reason I'm excited is that I'm as likely to be transformed by the experience as anyone else. I may play a leadership role alongside a number of others, but ultimately I'm a participant in something much greater than any of us is facilitating.

I haven't always felt this way about worship. I've served as senior pastor of Scottsdale Congregational UCC (SCUCC) for ten years now, and while the first five years were meaningful and substantive, the last five have really gotten my heart pumping.[1]

What changed? Our understanding of worship changed. With a change in understanding has come change in practice. Contrary to what some might expect, the form of worship has not changed from "traditional" to "contemporary" so much as from "message-based" to "incarnational."

By message-based worship I mean worship that is driven by an orally delivered sermon, set within a relatively fixed liturgy. Worship elements are essentially auditory in form, with visual elements primarily restricted to text printed on a page or screen for the purpose of corporate recitation. Other sensory elements are kept to a minimum lest they distract participants' attention from the delivery of the message.

By incarnational worship I mean worship that is driven by a series of multisensory experiences set within a highly flexible liturgy. Worship elements normally comprise a rich mixture of auditory, visual, kinesthetic, olfactory, and even gustatory forms. Nonauditory elements are not seen as distractions from the message, but as core components of an overall worship experience, which as a whole creates whatever message a person may take home. The goal of incarnational worship is less to teach people about God than to open people to experiencing God at the heart of their everyday lives and embodying their experience.

The quick way to tell if people have attended a message-based or an incarnational worship service is to listen in on what satisfied participants tell the pastor on the way out. If they say, "That was a great *sermon*," they have almost certainly been to a message-based service. If they say, "That was a great *service*," they have likely participated in incarnational worship.

Parishioners at SCUCC transitioning from exclaiming, "Great sermon!" to "Great service!" signified changes that had a significant, positive impact on nearly every other aspect of our ministry. More important, parishioners were much more likely to incorporate insights gleaned from their incarnational Sunday worship experience into their everyday lives outside of church. As a side benefit, our church has grown steadily these past five years, from two hundred to three hundred members, with the majority of growth coming from the so-called unchurched population. Overall, our change in worship has pretty much changed everything else with it.

The World's Most Dangerous Bible Study

The transformation in worship at SCUCC began with a Bible study— a wacky one at that. During my first year at SCUCC, we started a Wednesday Logos program for children and youth. Logos is an ecumenical, nationwide program that goes by different names in churches (ours is called B.E.A.C.H.).[2] The basic program contains four elements: Bible study, worship skills, recreation, and dinner. The program is run primarily by laity.

Just before our program started, there was one gaping hole: no one had come forward to lead Bible study for our middle and high school youth. Since I had just arrived from Princeton Theological Seminary fresh from my Ph.D. studies in the Hebrew Bible, all heads turned to me. "Eric, how would you like to lead Bible study for the middle and high school groups?" someone asked. I was just naive enough at the time to answer, "Sure, I'd love to! I've never taught youth before. It sounds like fun."

I was pretty excited about the whole thing until I met the youth themselves and assessed their interest in, and commitment to, studying the Bible at somewhere less than zero! Panic set in.

I don't particularly like using prepackaged curricula to teach any form of class, but in this case I was so desperate I sorted through piles of published youth-oriented Bible studies. Much to my dismay, I found them to be utterly boring or overly conservative, or both. So I cleared them off my desk, got down on my knees, and prayed. Hard!

I asked God, "What is at the center of our youth's world?" I figured that if I could discern what is at the center, I could step into it, on their own turf, bringing scriptures along with me, letting them speak naturally within the world of our youth.

It didn't take me long to figure out that if anything is at the center, music is part of it—rock, pop, alternative, rap, even country music for some. Happily, at the time I was listening to much of the same music, which emboldened me to step into the center of their world using music as our common meeting place.

I started something that has become known as *The World's Most Dangerous Bible Study* (WMDBS).[3] Each week we would focus on a particular song and one or two Scripture passages. My criteria for selecting a song was simple: (1) are the youth currently listening to it, and (2) does it express anything meaningful about life? Theologically, I assumed that if a song expresses anything meaningful about life, there must be a way of engaging with it fruitfully in Scripture.

Having selected a song, we would play it on a boom box (usually at high decibel levels!), following along with lyrics I had printed for the group in advance. When the song was over, I would ask, "What are the major thoughts, emotions, and messages you find in the song?" Responses would be written on a white board behind me.

Then we would turn to one or two Scripture passages I had chosen in advance. We would read each passage, then ask the same questions we had of the song, noting responses on the white board.

Finally, after discussing both the song and the scriptures in isolation, we would set them in conversation, asking, "What similarities and differences do we find between the song and the scriptures?"

The purpose of the WMDBS was not to say, "Look at your evil, devil music compared to the great and awesome scriptures." Nor was it to say, "You see, it all just says the same thing anyway (so why read the Bible?)." Rather, its purpose was to engage faith and everyday life using the Bible and popular music as conversation partners.

Can you imagine what happened? It worked! By "worked" I primarily mean three things:

1. The youth actually showed up each week, rather than every once in a while—when they had nothing "better" to do.

2. The youth often brought friends—sometimes even their "significant others."[4]
3. Most important, the youth got it.

By "got it" I do not mean to imply that when they hear, say, Alanis Morissette's "You Learn" on the radio, they think of Romans 8:28-39, which I had paired with this particular song. Rather, I mean that when the youth hear a song we covered in the WMDBS, they remember. They remember that faith engaged the heart of their everyday lives in a fruitful way—in a way that mattered very personally to them.

Once our youth understood the relationship between faith and everyday life, the wheels started spinning. Rapidly. They wanted to get more involved in church. They started attending other church functions and events. They volunteered to teach Sunday school. They helped with church mission projects.

Yet despite our youths' newfound enthusiasm for seemingly everything having to do with church, there was one place the youth absolutely would not go. Worship. They avoided worship like you or I would stay clear of a nuclear reactor meltdown.

"Is worship *that bad?*" us older folks asked. At the time, we had a single, traditional service at 10:00 Sunday mornings. And no, worship really wasn't *that bad.* By any other measure, the service appeared to be doing just fine. It enjoyed broad congregational support. It had lots of energy. It was growing—not rapidly, but steadily enough that we knew we would be forced to start a second service within the next couple of years to accommodate everyone. Our youth were the only ones not coming.

The Plum That Became a Hand Grenade

I fretted over our lack of youth participation in worship. I fretted particularly since I couldn't simply do what churches typically train you to do: blame the youth themselves. After all, the youth had proven beyond doubt to be highly interested and willing to participate in areas where they readily found a connection to their everyday lives.

One day I was driving home from church listening to music on my car's CD player. As I continued to puzzle over our lack of youth involvement, a "plum fell from heaven," as the Buddhists say. The "plum" took the form of an inner observation: "Eric, this happens every week. You pull into church, turning off the rock or jazz on your CD player, then go inside and offer what you have to offer. Afterward, you pull away from church, turning back on your rock or jazz, and that's where it stays all week long."

"Yes," I thought, "that's pretty accurate."

Another "plum" fell, taking the form of a question: "Does the music you listen to all week long move you spiritually?"

"Yes, definitely," I responded. "If it didn't, I wouldn't be listening to it all week."

A final "plum" fell, which I experienced more like a hand grenade: "If you're listening to this music all week long, and if it's moving you spiritually like you say, then why is there a firewall around worship? Why aren't you bringing it into the sanctuary, especially when your congregation isn't listening to 'church music' during the week either?"

I could not answer this question. I had no idea why music or, for that matter, any number of other elements from everyday life were held at bay at the doors of the sanctuary. Frankly, I had never seriously considered it a problem before. I am a child of traditional, mainline Protestantism. So-called traditional worship makes sense to me.[5] I relate to the hymns, the liturgy, the sermon. Yet as much as I love these things, I must admit that neither I nor the majority of my congregation listens to "traditional" worship music during the rest of the week, nor do we have much interest in reciting responsive readings or listening to more sermons outside Sunday mornings.

I thought about all the complaining we ministers and academics do about how good church folks in the mainline church don't seem to bring Sunday morning into the rest of the week. Could it be that the problem is not the failure of our laity to bring Sunday morning forward to Monday afternoon, but the failure of church leaders to bring Monday into Sunday? I suppose there is some sort of "splendid isolation" one can feel about stepping into worship that looks very little like everyday life, but at what cost? At the cost of everyday life itself?

I was so distressed about these questions that the very next day I called our music director and youth leader, Alan Murray, asking him to help me think through these issues. As a result of our conversations and a little fund-raising from a few families in the congregation, a handful of youth and adult leaders launched a monthly worship service for teenagers that became known as Alt.Faith.

Worship as Experimental Laboratory

Our basis for starting Alt.Faith was not only to do something wonderful for our youth, but to test out a hunch that has since become one of our foundational pieces of worship theory. The theory is this: bring everyday life into the heart of worship, and people will bring worship into the heart of their everyday lives. Life itself will ultimately become an act of worship.

Alt.Faith thus served as an experimental laboratory for what worship for all ages might look like in the future. We found that with youth we could really push the envelope. We could try all kinds of new ideas that might prove to be complete disasters if inflicted upon our "traditional" folk. We could take risks, working on little more than hunches and intuitions, knowing that we could either succeed wildly or—just as important—fail miserably and not lose half our congregation and budget along with it.

Through Alt.Faith we tried all kinds of experiments. We hired a rock band who did not know "church music." We experimented with multimedia—something about which I'd previously sworn, "Hell will freeze over before I ever use it in worship." The sermon became like a World's Most Dangerous Bible Study on steroids. Youth brought in poetry and quotes from books they had been reading. We drew on a wide variety of arts, including drama and dance. Whatever we brought in, we were determined not to let it be used as mere "religitainment," but to make it core, message-bearing material. We invited all of life into the dance of faith.

During the two years of Alt.Faith's existence, we experienced a number of wild successes and miserable failures. Both! Yet looking back, it really did not matter whether we failed or succeeded each month because, either way, we learned something we did not know previously about worship.

Our greatest finding was that the original hunch was absolutely correct. You *can* bring everyday life into worship in such a way that worship goes back into everyday life. Worship in this mode is capable of reframing life, setting the human story into deep relationship with God's larger story. When this happens, the dividing line between the sacred and profane becomes quite fuzzy. One discovers the sacred within what was once thought to be profane, and the profane itself is readily transformed by the sacred.

Sometimes people would ask how we could bring secular music or non-Christian art forms into church. I would respond, "Just open your Bible and you'll find your answer." If the Psalms can affirm that the seas, hills, and forests are all capable of praising and glorifying God though they be inanimate objects without minds or souls, how much more can human beings do these same things without being consciously aware of what they are doing. It simply takes the lens of faith to perceive it. We discovered in Alt.Faith that worship can provide such a lens.

From Alt.Faith to The Studio

Based on what we learned from Alt.Faith and an increasingly crowded sanctuary on Sunday mornings, we set about crafting a second weekly Sunday morning service that eventually became known as The Studio. Rather than being a replica of our "traditional" service, The Studio was intended specifically to resonate with all ages, including youth, and to serve as an outreach to the so-called unchurched population.

In the midst of our initial planning process for this future service, another "plum" fell from heaven. This one ended up having at least as great an impact on the formation of The Studio as the three previous "plums" had on Alt.Faith.

I had been reading Annie Dillard's *Pilgrim at Tinker Creek* while on summer study leave at a small, lakeside cabin on the southern Oregon coast. Dillard's reflections on God's mysterious hand in nature proved to be so captivating that instead of closing my eyes during my early morning meditations, I would keep them wide open.

One morning I was meditating at the end of our cabin's dock, peering through the surface of the water to the sandy bottom below. I was looking at nothing in particular but rather was using the stillness of the scene to quiet my soul enough to ponder a question I had come to Oregon hoping to answer. The question was deceptively simple: what is the basis of worship? Since SCUCC had decided not to make its second service a replica of the first, we felt the need to go back to the drawing board, considering the most fundamental building blocks of worship before moving forward.

While deep in reflection, I suddenly sensed motion at the periphery of my vision. My eyes adjusted their focus just in time to behold the largest bass I have ever seen shoot right past me. The bass was so big that, though it was swimming next to the sand three feet below the surface, it was causing ripples on top. I stood up and gasped as a sense of awe and wonder provoked a surge of adrenaline through my body.

The moment after I gasped, the "plum" dropped. This "plum" took the form of an insight, which essentially went like this: "This is the foundation of worship. If you can take that hour or so you have on Sunday morning and open people to experiencing just a quarter second of the awe and wonder you just experienced, it is accomplished. You can pack up and go home. You have an hour or so for a quarter second."

I didn't know what to make of this insight at first, although something about it felt so intuitively correct that I trusted its import would eventually become clear. What perplexed me most was the thought of trying to manufacture an experience of the Divine in worship. How could it be done? If it were possible, would it not be overly manipulative to do so? The last thing I wanted was to create a service based simply on tugging people's emotions one way or another and pretending it was a God experience.

I took the insight and the questions surrounding it back with me to SCUCC, where a small team of us wrestled with the issues. After a bit of discussion and not a little prayer, we concluded that the object is not to *create* anything. Rather, the goal is simply to invite people into a sense of openness and attentiveness akin to sitting at the edge of that dock in Oregon. You never know whether or not a bass will swim by, but if one does, you want to be ready for it.

Theologically, we assumed that the Spirit of the living Christ is alive and well in this world and is fully present in worship. We also assumed that if a person opens up the tiniest crack in his or her heart, the Spirit will not hesitate to jump inside, stirring the deepest waters of the soul. Not all experiences may provoke an adrenaline rush like the bass did. Some may experience the stirrings of the Spirit in subtle, almost undetectable ways that only become clear in hindsight. In any case, we assumed that our job as worship leaders is to assist people in opening up the cracks in their hearts that may allow the Spirit to work. Teaching and intellect would play a strong role, as they do in message-based worship, but everything would be subservient to opening people to *experience.*

Thus, the basic platform for The Studio was born. We took the key insight gleaned from Alt.Faith—that if you bring everyday life into the heart of worship, worship will go out with you into the heart of your everyday life—and added the insight that worship should be centered more around *experience* than *message.* The result has been equivalent to pouring gasoline on a fire.

So what does The Studio practice of worship look like? The short answer is that you have to experience it for yourself to really get it. However, some description can be made.

The Studio makes strong use of the arts as an avenue to experience. On any given Sunday, this may include live painting or sculpting during worship, dance, poetry reading, hands-on artistic creations by the congregation, drama, film clips, multimedia reflections, performance art, and so on. We regularly draw on rock music in our multimedia reflections, though our base musical form is an improvisational form of jazz played by a professional jazz quintet. While most of the congregation never would have called themselves jazz lovers at the start (some, in fact, thought they "hated" jazz), we all have found that improvisational jazz suits experiential context particularly well. Hymns are scored in jazz, jazz improvisation is used to interpret Scripture and poetry readings, and jazz meditational forms underlie guided meditations and other contemplative prayer exercises, which are used frequently.[5]

In addition, participants may be invited to do journaling during the course of worship or enter into a dialogue individually or as a group with a worship leader. All this is planned and facilitated by a worship team made up primarily of laypeople who meet for three hours each week to share a meal, have fellowship, and engage in worship planning.[7]

There is no fixed liturgy in The Studio. It varies every week depending on the kind of experience to which we are trying to open people. While anyone familiar with Reformed worship style would recognize classic moves being made (gathering, confession, and so on), these moves appear in different order and radically different forms every week.

There is no formal sermon at The Studio. Although preaching takes place, it is normally broken up into three- to five-minute segments surrounded by other experiential elements. The pastor thus acts more as an interpretive guide through the service, reflecting on what just happened or providing an intellectual bridge between components.

If the theme for the morning is, for example, God as Creator, our worship team asks themselves, "How can we help open people to experiencing God as Creator during the time we have together, or at a bare minimum, model what an experience of our Creator God might be like?"

When we held a Studio service on the "God as Creator" theme, we focused on Genesis 2, where God sculpts human beings from the clay of the earth. When people entered worship, they were given pieces of clay to mold as they wished during most of the service. We also invited a local artist to sculpt a human figure during the course of the service so that even when the focus was not on the sculpting, it was still interacting subtly with everything we did.[8]

At various points I entered into dialogue with the sculptor about the practice of sculpting, noting connections between the sculpting process and Christian spirituality. For instance, one thing we learned is that sculptors use metal armatures under their clay figures so that the human form can be set in position without collapsing. A beginning sculptor uses a fairly rigid armature that has the benefit of holding the figure up but also restricts the variety of positions the figure can take. As a sculptor gains experience, gaining greater understanding of the delicate balance between form and gravity, thinner, more flexible armatures are used, allowing the experienced sculptor to set the figure in more interesting and graceful positions that will not collapse. What a metaphor for the spiritual path!

Later in the service we invited the congregation to reflect on what gifts God has given them that they may not be integrating currently in their daily lives. We invited people to pray that God would help them make better use of these gifts while molding the clay into a receptacle for their prayer. These pieces were brought forward to the altar during communion (which is held each week). We later fired the clay and assembled the pieces into a grand collage that stood at the entrance to the sanctuary for many weeks, reminding people of their prayers.

In the past we have called The Studio an experiential service. However, it is more accurate to call it an *incarnational worship experience*. By bringing everyday life into worship and centering worship around experiencing God at the heart of our everyday lives, the effect is that Spirit ultimately takes on flesh and blood, much like a sculptor's armature is ultimately covered in clay. People leave worship with solid tools for putting faith into practice beyond Sunday morning on much deeper levels than if we were content to simply let words and a few songs carry the content.

Crosstalk: Interplay between Services

So great has been the influence of The Studio form of worship that it has influenced our "traditional" worship in wonderful ways. While we still follow a classic Reformed liturgical format, we have learned that our "traditional" people love it when we integrate more experiential elements as well, including multimedia, artistic creation (by the congregation and by guest artists), and contemplative exercises.

Recently we made a change to our music format at the "traditional" service as well. Because of our rich experience with professional jazz musicians at The Studio at 11:00 a.m., we decided to make use of professional classical musicians at the 9:00 a.m. service. We hired the accompanist for the Phoenix Symphony to play piano and organ, and modified our choir program to include choir offerings twice a month rather than every week. On the nonchoir Sundays, we hire a guest musician or two, normally also from the symphony, to accompany our pianist.[9]

The result is that music at both services is now "through the roof," only in different realms. And when added to the other experiential elements we regularly weave into the "traditional" service, this service has attained a critical "experiential" mass and has begun to grow in spirit and numbers like The Studio. It is rapidly becoming as incarnational in its "traditional" format as The Studio is in its more "contemporary" form.

Ripples That Make Waves

Finally, I should mention one other important effect of our incarnational worship practice. When we started The Studio, we realized we wanted to grow smaller even as we grew larger. We thus set out with the goal of starting twenty "Oasis groups" in our (then) two hundred–member congregation. An Oasis group is made up of people who gather to explore literally any area of interest as long as they are interested in relating their interest to their faith. Examples include a film discussion group, a hiking group, a gardening group, an open and affirming group (gay, lesbian, bisexual, and transgendered issues), a spiritual explorations group, and so on.

Because worship and these affinity groups both are centered on the task of integrating faith experientially with everyday life, our worship ministry and our small group ministry intersect quite often. Sometimes Oasis groups form as a result of an experience people have had in worship. At other times Oasis groups themselves participate in worship.

As these groups have grown in size and numbers, they now make up a significant piece of the organizational vitality of the church. We continue to maintain traditional church boards and committees, but much of the day-to-day work of the church takes place naturally through the Oasis groups. Thus, for instance, the gardening group has participated in a beautification project sponsored by the board of trustees. The film group has teamed up with the open and affirming group to host a film series on justice issues in the glbt community. The missions group has joined with the Christian education board to host a youth mission trip to Mexico. When they returned, their experiences in Mexico were integrated into worship services focusing on poverty issues.

Truly, worship has changed everything at Scottsdale Congregational UCC. It took five years from the initial seeds sown in the World's Most Dangerous Bible Study to become a full-fledged Tree of Life (or Christmas Tree!) bearing gifts to our congregation and the wider community, but it has been worth every ounce of energy expended. People no longer see worship as taking place on Sunday only. Because worship has become incarnational—freely naming and claiming where the living Christ may be found in everyday life and establishing experiential connections to this Christ—our everyday life as a church and as individuals has become more incarnational. And this is the greatest gift of all.

Notes

1. One of our thirtysomething mothers summed up well the difference between "then and now" when she observed, "My husband and I used to come just for the sake of our kids. *Now* we come for us."

2. Our youth named the program after its first year. The name stands for Bible, Education and Activities in our Church Home.

3. Examples of the WMDBS have been published in the first four volumes of *Cloud of Witnesses*, an audio journal of Princeton Theological Seminary's Institute for Youth Ministry. Audio segments and sample lesson plans are available at the institute's website: www.ptsem.edu/iym.

4. The first time two of the girls brought their boyfriends to our Bible study, I nearly fell off my chair. I felt like Simeon in Luke 4: "Take me now, Lord, for I have seen your glory!"

5. I generally place quotes around both "traditional" and "contemporary" when used as adjectives for worship. Often when people refer to "traditional" worship, they are not referring to worship that goes very far back in Christian history at all. Normally, they are referring to whatever form of worship was in vogue when they or their pastor were in seminary. On the other hand, what is "contemporary"? Many "contemporary" services don't seem very contemporary to me, but rather refried versions of 1970s or 80s youth camp services. And really, can't any form of worship—even very ancient forms— legitimately be called "contemporary" as long as they are able to help people in contemporary times connect with the living Word of God?

6. For more on how we use jazz in worship, visit Chuck Marohnic's website at www.chuckmarohnic.com. See also *Igniting Worship: The Seven Deadly Sins* by Eric Elnes (Nashville: Abingdon, 2004).

7. For more on the formation, care, and feeding of a worship team, see Elnes, *Igniting Worship*, 25–29.

8. We now regularly make use of a live camera feed projected on one of our two screens that intensifies the interplay between artistic creation and other elements of the service.

9. We did this for no more money than we had been spending before to hire a weekly choir director.

Proclaiming God's Word

Practicing What We Preach

Timothy Shapiro
Westminster Presbyterian Church
Xenia, Ohio

Westminster Presbyterian Church is located in Xenia, Ohio, a typical Midwestern town famous mostly for its destruction in 1974 by a massive tornado. In this place, as in churches across the country, the minister and members found themselves looking for a way to connect preaching on Sunday with everyday life. So they adopted a practice of gathering roundtable groups with the preacher to discuss sermon ideas in light of how Christian practice looks in everyday life. Through this shared reflection, Westminster has discovered that preaching is not only exegeting Scripture but exegeting life. And as Timothy Shapiro shares in this essay, this realization has helped the congregation both to practice what is preached and to preach from the wisdom of its practice.

Picture a town in Ohio. Not just any town, a particular place called Xenia. This town has a beautiful park, tree-lined streets, and many people who are lifelong friends. In 1974 a tornado, or as some claim, three tornadoes, devastated the town. Longtime residents of Xenia mark their lives before and after this date. The Weather Channel regularly broadcasts a documentary about that April day. If you call L.L. Bean to order a sweater, the salesperson says, "Xenia—I've heard of that place."

Now imagine people from the Westminster Presbyterian Church walking into a room on a Sunday evening. Blue carpet, a flock of chairs, and a fireplace mark the room. The first arrivals arrange the chairs in a semicircle. Soon the rest of the group arrives. There's Paula, a retired city administrator; Ann, a young architect; Ben, a CFO; Tom, a graduate student in psychology; and three other members as well as Nevin, a pastor from Kenya. During the meeting they discuss how they live their faith. They talk about how they practice what they preach.

We often urge people to practice what they preach when there is a gap between what they say and what they do. We note the physician who smokes, the education professor who mumbles in class, or the banker whose finances are a mess.

Preachers, too, are susceptible to this indictment. Preachers say such beautiful words during worship, yet often their lives do not match the measure of their language. The preachers' burden is that their lives are never as exquisite as their finest proclamation.

Congregations have their own challenges living the gospel. Boards work months editing the words of a vision statement so that the assertion soars close to heaven. Yet the rhetoric crashes to earth when the fellowship hall roof leaks. An elder gets miffed because the board ignores the repair estimate from his nephew.

Is there a way for preachers and listeners to experience a closer connection between the words of faith and the actions of everyday life? What if the phrase "Practice what you preach" was not so much indictment as encouragement?

In the Reformed tradition, the creation of the sermon is not typically a collaborative process. The pastor creates the sermon. Why? Because someone has to do it. When the congregation assembles for worship, a pastor preaches so that things don't descend into chaos. Imagine hearing, "Who is preaching this Sunday?" "I don't know, let's draw straws!"

Yet, at Westminster, Xenia, the sermon is developed from a conversation between the pastor and members who rotate in and out of a small group. As Paula says while sitting in that blue-carpeted room, "I'm dying to know how my friends in the pew live their faith."

So picture a preacher in a room with seven church members and a visitor from Kenya. They have gathered to talk about a life activity—in this case, the way friendship functions in their lives. They have read articles on friendship. They have studied scriptures on friendship. Soon they will share stories of the challenge and grace of friendship.

Practicing what one preaches mixes two disciplines: a collaborative preaching method and a practical theology of living faith. Collaborative preaching makes use of sermon roundtable groups, a small group of people gathered to talk about ideas for next week's sermon. The group focuses on a particular life activity, for instance, friendship or hospitality or household economics. During conversation the activity is juxtaposed with scripture passages. Participants then brainstorm content for the sermon that will concentrate on, in this case, friendship. They will also reflect on their participation in this particular activity.

Preaching on life activities changes the kind of conversations that take place among members of a congregation. Such preaching does not guarantee twice as many people in worship or debate about mission giving that is free from discomfort. It does shift the nature of things about which people talk. Members of the congregation become less focused on "in-church" issues (the color of the carpet) and more attentive to deeper engagement with the world. As the conversation changes, people tend to find more options regarding how to integrate faith into their daily life. As the group's extrovert, Paula, says, "God is shared. The Bible belongs to us all. These activities aren't just one person's. Doesn't faithful interpretation depend on us all working together?"

The sermon roundtable was developed by John S. McClure, who describes a collaborative method of preaching in his book *The Roundtable Pulpit: Where Leadership and Preaching Meet.*[1] In McClure's model, discussion of a lectionary text drives the conversation. The model I'm describing differs from McClure's in that the group discusses a life activity first, then considers scripture.

Participants not only brainstorm content for the sermon, they also reflect on their participation in the activity. The roundtable conversation lets participants practice particular life activities in relationship to their faith. The leader introduces a Bible passage and asks, "How does this passage link with our conversation?" Before the end of the meeting, agreements develop regarding ideas and behaviors concerning the life activity. The proposals resist a "one size fits all" view. The ideas and behaviors are tentative. They take into account a variety of life experiences. During the week, e-mails pass back and forth. The conversation continues in the grocery and at the beginning of the worship team meeting. In this process, scripture and even the sermon become a kind of inscribed practice. That is, words about the activity are embodied as congregants try new ways of behaving in light of what they have heard from the pulpit. Once the sermon is preached, the entire congregation, not just the roundtable group, has the opportunity to think more deeply and act more consciously regarding the life activity.

My pattern for the small group conversation is similar to the shared praxis model developed by Thomas Groome in *Christian Religious Education: Sharing Our Story and Vision.*[2] It involves five segments or sweeps of conversation. Each sweep takes the group deeper into the chosen topic. The pattern of the sweeps looks like this:

Sweep 1: The present practice. Group members tell of their own experience regarding the particular practice. For example, "Now, most of my friends are from work."

Sweep 2: Critical reflection. Group members engage in critical reflection of their present experience. For instance, "I wonder if I'm not open to new people in my life because everything revolves around work."

Sweep 3: Scripture. The roundtable encounters Bible texts they generate or texts generated by the preacher that relate to the activity under consideration. Constellations of texts are studied. The group places their conversation within a wider network of theological understanding. Someone says, "I remember more hymns about Jesus being our friend than Bible passages."

Sweep 4: Tension between scripture and practice. The group places their understanding and actions regarding an activity over and against what they understand to be the scriptural witness toward the activity. What does the text mean for our practice of the faith? What affirmations do we see? What disconnects exist? A group member might observe, "When congregations are stressed they aren't the friendliest of places."

Sweep 5: Decision and response. How will we change our practice? Can we appropriate these behaviors into our everyday life? Can we encourage other members of the congregation to join?

On Sunday the pastor preaches a sermon reflecting the conversation concerning the activity. The sermon is more than a journalistic report. The preacher has made editorial and rhetorical decisions that engage not only those who were present at the small group, but the rest of the congregation as well. Though the preacher uses a variety of preaching forms, the sweep of the small group conversation provides one model of how the sermon might develop.

For three more weeks, the small group continues to meet to talk about the juxtaposition of friendship and Scripture. When the month is over, another small group in the congregation will take up another life activity (hospitality, generosity, Sabbath keeping, etc.) and follow the same pattern.

People often say they want a sermon to connect faith to everyday life. They seek sermons that address experiences at home and at work and sermons that address what they hear in the news. They seek words that will help them make sense of encounters with people and places different from the familiar. In his book *The Monday Connection*, William Diehl speaks of joining a church as an adult. He finds the people open and friendly. Worship is lively. Nevertheless, a problem exists. Diehl writes, "My Sunday experience had no connection to my Monday world. The worlds that came to me from the Bible and the pulpit made no sense to me in my weekday world."[3] What if the sermon did help people make sense of their weekday world? What if the sermon also helped people act more consciously from their faith?

Back at the blue-carpeted room, the roundtable group begins their Sunday evening discussion. Paula tells of her elementary school teacher, Miss Kerr. "She taught us reading, writing, and arithmetic," Paula says. "And she taught us to be friends. She would stop in the middle of the lesson, standing at the chalkboard, and say to us, 'You students need to be friends to each other.' She taught us this not only by telling us we needed to be friends but also by acting like a friend toward us. She was the kindest person I knew growing up." Paula observes that in a one-room school, friendships crossed age barriers and power barriers.

The group wonders whether work roles limit friendships. Can a teacher be a friend to his students? Can a doctor befriend her patients? Can a minister befriend parishioners?

Margaret, a nursing home social director, asks, "What about Jesus? Is it possible for Jesus to have a friend? How can the Almighty be a friend to us mortals? It doesn't seem balanced."

The group offers different words to describe unbalanced friendships: codependent relationships, friendships that have a lot of should haves and could haves. The group settles on the idea that friendships, like all human relationships, are inherently out of balance. No aspect of life is in equilibrium.

Ann, an architect, says, "We've been told we can have it all, that we can balance our work, our marriage, and our life as parents. This is not my experience. If I pay attention to my kids—as they deserve—I have to give up something at work. Those who claim we can have it all in balance are not telling the truth."

Margaret turns the pages of her Bible. She says, "I've been looking for this. Can I read?"

Ann says, "This is a good time to hear a passage." Margaret reads John 15:12-17. For the group, verse 15 is a key line: "I do not call you servants any longer, because the servant does not know what the master is doing; but I have called you friends, because I have made known to you everything that I have heard from my Father" (NRSV).

Nevin says that in his village in Kenya serving another person isn't seen as a negative thing because no one has status over another. However, he says that in the United States he isn't comfortable with the way the word *servant* is used. "I think," he says, "that people use power as a way to protect themselves from others."

Margaret says, "That's why I chose John 15. Jesus' comments about friends and servants sound parallel to the topic of balance in friendships."

Here is how some of the conversation is captured in the sermon preached to the congregation the following Sunday:

> *You are my friends, when you do what I command.*
> *I do not call you servants any longer. I call you friends.*

The word *servant* has too much of a "what I owe you" connotation to it. Servant can be framed too easily in terms of the economics of relationships. Therefore, Jesus does not want that word associated with his disciples. Servants are not only treated "unequal" to their masters, they are not free. Moreover, servants are not expected to gain any pleasure out of this unequal relationship. But Jesus does not have servants—not in this sense. He has no desire to shield himself from others. Pharaoh may have servants. The Roman Empire may have servants. Big corporations may have servants. But not Jesus. Jesus has friends. Friends may be unequally yoked, have different incomes, gifts, and unequal sources of power, but in a friendship, people are free.

I do not call you servants any longer. I call you friends.

These are unexpected words. Maybe we have been desensitized by hymns like "What a Friend We Have in Jesus" and are no longer astonished that God would be our friend. . . . No relationship is equal. Friendships are inherently unstable. I need you. Then, lo and behold, you need me. But hardly ever equally. Though friendships are unbalanced, what marks a friendship is not so much shared power as it is shared pleasure.

I told you how one of our church members recalls a teacher who taught friendship along with reading, writing, and arithmetic.

She taught friendship by befriending her students. You know that a teacher/student relationship is not equal. It cannot be. Teachers have more power than students do. Nevertheless, there can be a shared pleasure in the learning relationship.

Years ago when this teacher was long retired, well into her eighties she would receive the phone call, the personal invitation, to the annual class reunion. The class treated this teacher like a jewel even though she now was no longer their teacher. Sitting at the table at the class reunion, surrounded by iced tea and dessert, what could she have felt except a kind of joy that can never be paid or earned, only given.

I do not call you students any longer, I call you friends.

Ben arrives late for the next meeting. "Board conference call." he says.

He tries to take a seat behind the others, but Paula stops him. "Nope," she says, "we are all in this together."

I ask the group if they have any recent experiences of friendship they want to share with the group. Ann says that she is designing an office for a group of physicians. "I know nothing about the world of physicians. These men and women are so smart and just a bit quiet. So I have to figure out what they mean when they answer a question with two words."

Ben asks, "Are they friends?"

"No," says Ann. "In fact it works better if I don't try to be their friend."

"See," says Margaret, "this is what I meant last week by unbalanced relationships. Are we supposed to be everyone's friend? We sang that hymn on Sunday. A cappella, it sounded nice. But think if the song was, 'What a Stranger We Have in Jesus'?"

The group meets for two more weeks. They continue to share stories and place those experiences next to Scripture. During their meetings, the group talks about all kinds of issues related to friendship, faith, and Scripture. The following comments are captured in sermons:

- "Almost all practices are closely linked to friendship. For example, the practices of hospitality and forgiveness correspond to relationships."
- "We meet Jesus in the holy space between good friends."
- "The Emmaus Road story provides a model on why every stranger can be viewed as a potential friend."
- "Friendships can protect us against evil (e.g., the story of David and Jonathan)."
- "A spiritual kinship exists between being with friends and being with Jesus."

The final roundtable meeting is delayed for a week when a tornado races through Xenia the Thursday before the final meeting. The tornado kills one person, destroys dozens of homes, damages many businesses, and blows down four churches. This is the third major tornado in Xenia since the big storm of 1974. The Westminster building isn't damaged. However, the homes of several church members are left without roofs and in a few cases some are no longer standing.

When the roundtable meets after the delay, the group has tornado stories to tell. A church member pulled a child from under a collapsed church wall. Someone was up all night checking neighborhood gas lines. People received e-mails and phone calls from friends as far away as Australia. Friends comforted friends by staying up all night with them when tornado warnings sounded a few days after the storm. Paula led a phone chain project for Westminster. Everyone associated with the congregation was called. "How are you? Can the church help? Let's all be in worship this Sunday."

During the first part of the roundtable, people tell stories of best friends helping best friends. Someone at the roundtable remembers that the previous sermon asserted that if we want to know how Jesus Christ might respond in any given situation, we should picture the healthy response of a best friend. The group reads two selections from Scripture. I choose one, Proverbs 14:10 as paraphrased by Eugene Peterson, "The person who shuns the bitter moments of friends will be an outsider at their celebrations" (MESSAGE). Marie, a retired schoolteacher, chooses another; Mark 2:1-12, the story of the paralytic brought to Jesus by four people.

The group seems ready to move past the tornado stories. A new theme involves the relationship between faith and friendship. Marie carries the group in this direction when she says, "I'm thinking of a saying that goes something like, 'God can't be a friend without us.'"

Marie tells about a friend, Loraine, who battles a tough cancer. Marie says, "Loraine gets us all together. We sew. We cut out fabrics. We make hats in different sizes for others going through chemotherapy. She has a fierce determination to do something for others who are sick. We are carrying people who are carrying people."

Ben shares feedback from a congregational member. The member is troubled by the tone of the sermons. She told Ben that she doesn't buy the positive picture of friendships. "My experience with friendship has been much more disappointing than what I'm hearing from you all," the church member tells Ben. She says, "People who I thought were my best friends have hurt me deeply."

No one speaks right away. They are thinking.

After awhile, Ann says, "I am in an unbalanced friendship, and I end up very angry that I allowed it to happen."

Ben agrees, "Yes, our friends help us to be Christian."

Aaron, a retired chemist as well as a sturdy lay theologian, alludes to some who say that not only do our friends help us be Christian, but also that it is impossible to be Christian without friends. He argues along the lines of some theologians who say that Christian friendship is a prerequisite for Christian practice and faith.

Paula and Tom (a young adult in graduate school) want to moderate what sounds like a legal expectation of friendship. Paula says, "Friendships seem to be formed more by things like intuition. I don't think you can say friendship is required for faith. Both faith and friendship are more from the heart of a special kind of knowing."

Tom quotes a hymn: "From sorrow, toil and pain, and sin, we shall be free; and perfect love and friendship reign through eternity." Tom has a point to make: "I can think of people who would have a hard time with making friends, but I still would consider them Christian. I mean, what about the trucker who prays every day to Jesus but is on the road so much that it's hard for him to have friendships? Or the pope? I'm not sure a person in what we might call high places would be able to nurture deep friendships. There must be loneliness for people who have lots of responsibility. So I'm not sure the pope has friends, but would we say the pope is not Christian? I'm thinking of monks who live by themselves, hermits, who take a vow of silence or live in isolation—would they not be Christian?"

Here is a portion of the sermon developed from this conversation:

> Friends carry each other in so many ways. The tornado hits at night. One of our church members is out of town. There's a hole in this member's home near the roof. The hole is temporarily repaired at 1:00 in the morning by a friend, another member of Westminster. Friendships consist of acts of kindness that involve sacrifice that do not feel like sacrifice.
>
> Friends carry each other in many ways. One of us has a friend diagnosed with cancer. This friend is determined to live life fully. She collects her friends together and they form a sewing group. They talk. They joke. They sew hats—yes, hats—together. These hats are for people losing their hair from chemotherapy.
>
> Now some Christian scholars go as far as to say that you must have friends in order to be Christian. Some scholars, in an effort to be provocative, say that you really can't read the Bible or pray without friends. At the roundtable, some of us resisted this thought. Some of us believed this kind of thinking made the gift of friendship into a law. There are those among us who have a high value for friends, but this isn't the direction they want to go. Can someone in a position of high responsibility really have friends? Does, for instance, the pope have friends? Would we really say the pope isn't Christian because his position of power secludes him? Or what about the truck driver who is right now somewhere in Missouri listening to a radio preacher while he says his prayers—alone—as he drives. He's on the road. He's divorced. He prays but has no

best friends. Most of us in the group felt that such a person does live the Christian faith.

Rather than say that you must have friends in order to be Christian, it is more accurate to say that friendships, as gifts, can be valuable places to practice our faith. When the relationship is working, friendships bring out the best of our Christian faith. This is more gift than achievement.

You might be interested to know, though, that the roundtable did talk about times when friendships were not so—well—friendly. One of us said, "I was in an unbalanced friendship, and I ended up being very disappointed that I allowed it to happen; and afterwards I was afraid because I didn't want to deal with all the bad feelings."

Are there others of you who have heard all our positive talk about friendship—friendship as the gateway to Christianity!—and wondered if anyone was going to fess up about the way friends sometimes break each other? Would this be at all like the experience of the paralyzed man *before* he was brought to the house— feeling stuck, feeling on the outside, wondering where he fit in?

Conversation from the roundtable starting with life activities helps the preaching event to connect more deeply with everyday issues. People are curious about the way others wrestle with practicing their faith. The roundtable sermons meet people in their curiosity. Participants thought more deeply about friendship. For instance, Paula thought longer and harder about reconnecting with her former teacher and classmates. Ann talked about renegotiating a friendship that she found difficult. Tom invited the group (and the congregation) to think more thoroughly about how one's vocation shapes relationships. Congregational members who listened to the sermons also addressed friendship more intentionally. The person who noted that her experience had not been all positive thanked the preacher for noting her comment because "I'm sure that others have shared my experience."

Preaching on practice in the collaborative model works well for the Sundays during Ordinary Time; the days of the church year that do not mark specific events in Christ's life. During Lent, Easter, Advent, and Christmas, Bible texts are oriented around key moments of Christ's mission. These texts focus on Christ's work. Ordinary time is an appropriate time to move the focus from Christ's story to ours.

The roundtable group focused on a practice deals with everyday experiences located at the intersection of faith and life. Many ideas and experiences are shared. At times it is difficult to organize the material into a coherent sermon. As with any sermon, it is important to edit out extraneous material, to be clear about the sermon's focus, and to make transitions clear. With this process, I am editing people's experiences (not just their ideas). I am not simply editing my own ideas, but events that mean something to others. It is possible, of course, that the experiences shared at the roundtable are too parochial. They do not push the margins. Sometimes the pastor will need to provide edgier opinions.

This collaborative method of developing a sermon will not magically change a congregation into a "model community of faith." However, this collaborative process connects a central part of congregational life, the sermon, with a central part of the Christian life, the community's everyday experience. The connection is made through sermons that exegete not only Bible texts, but also exegete life practice. Together, members of a faith community study the Bible and extend the story of Scripture. The message heard from the pulpit is a word that comes from the Bible and from the lived experience of parishioners; someone greets a stranger, another prepares for a reunion, a tornado blows through town. The Word of God is no longer out there, but is near. Practice preaching proclaims faith in such a way that the congregation can say, "We stand by this word." Or as Paul writes, "This is the Good News which we have received, by which we stand" (1 Cor. 15:1).[4]

Notes

1. John S. McClure, *The Roundtable Pulpit: Where Leadership and Preaching Meet* (Nashville: Abingdon, 1995), 24.
2. Thomas H. Groome, *Christian Religious Education: Sharing Our Story and Vision* (San Francisco: Jossey-Bass, 1999).

3. William E. Diehl, *The Monday Connection: On Being an Authentic Christian in a Weekday World* (San Francisco: Harper SanFrancisco, 1992), 10.

4. Adapted from an affirmation of faith found in *Book of Common Worship* (Louisville: Westminster John Knox, 1993), 96.

SPEAKING FAITH

Grace Breaking In

Lillian Daniel
Church of the Redeemer
New Haven, Connecticut

*Few locations are as genteel as that of Redeemer United Church of
Christ in New Haven, Connecticut, located just down the street
from Yale Divinity School. Yet, despite its proximity to this bastion
of New England Protestantism, Redeemer had fallen upon
difficult times. As Lillian Daniel, the church's former pastor,
shares in this essay, a remarkable transformation occurred when
the congregation seized on the practice of giving testimony, a
practice deeply rooted in the faith of its Puritan forebears but
intimidating to contemporary Congregationalists. By adapting this
old practice to a new culture, Redeemer began to resonate with the
stories of God at work in its midst and discovered many other
practices that were key to its identity and mission.*

As the Lenten season ran its course at our traditional-looking mainline Protestant church in New Haven, behind the clear glass windows, in the middle of our worship service, something unusual was
happening: we were hearing testimonies.

We have too many attorneys in the congregation to call these
communications "testimonies." For that matter, we have too many
people on the run from traditions who do call them "testimonies."
So at the Church of the Redeemer we call these statements made by

97

laypeople during church services "Lenten reflections." They do, however, fall under the category of Christian testimony.

About a year earlier, our church book group devoured *Practicing
the Faith*, edited by Dorothy Bass. We discussed one practice each
session, and the conversation was lively. Everybody wanted to hear
more about discernment and saying yes and saying no. These were
spiritual practices that could help with the busiest of lives. The chapter on Sabbath keeping was more challenging. Could this group keep
Sabbath and at the same time be leaders in a frenetically active Congregational church where we are always one step away from works
righteousness?

The chapter that drew the least conversation was the one by
Thomas Hoyt Jr. on testimony. Commenting on Hoyt's description
of how as a boy he was nurtured in the practice of testimony, members of the book group told stories of other people's churches where
testimonies were given, but clearly these churches were, to them, like
New York City—a nice place to visit, but you wouldn't want to live
there.

Hoyt's comments were not limited to just one Christian tradition. Where he laid out a vision of testimony beyond words, the
group came on board, immediately understanding how serving a meal
at a shelter was a form of testimony. But as for the descriptions of
speaking out loud about one's faith in worship, our group seemed to
read the chapter as if it were an anthropology article—an intriguing
description of what other people did.

Why not our church? I thought to myself.

As a minister in a congregation of creative and thoughtful people,
I have long been concerned that we ask for their gifts in all areas of
church life except worship. Certainly the singers and the readers have
their liturgical places, and for those who participate, those are rich
ministries. But what about the rest who might have stories to tell
that defy the church staff's ability to script?

Despite the book group's removed reaction to the practice of
testimony, I knew there was a hunger for this sort of opportunity,
because the church announcements were getting long again. People
who could have told you in thirty seconds where and when the com-

munity organizing meeting was were getting up and telling stories first.

Prayer requests were turning into small testimonies, as some people did not want to offer requests but stories about prayers that were answered. A prayer request on the anniversary of a mother's death might lead into a few lessons she had taught.

In addition, for the third year in a row, people were telling me that they looked forward to our stewardship season because they longed to hear church members offer "giving moments," which are, in effect, testimonies. In giving moments people tell stories about their walk with God through the life of our church. Sometimes the stories are funny. Sometimes people cry. As one member put it, "I love stewardship season because I get so excited about what people will say."

While no one would use the word, I sensed our congregation was hungry for testimony, and when I presented the idea to the deacons (who are the lay leaders responsible for the worship and spiritual life of the congregation), they agreed. But as leaders, we had to be creative about how we introduced this practice of the faith, carried out by Christians throughout history but not so often in the middle of worship at our own Church of the Redeemer.

So we had to introduce the practice while understanding our own church culture. The deacons came up with the phrase "Lenten Reflections," sensing that these were words the congregation would understand. Then we invited a few people we had not heard from before to prepare something in advance for five worship services during Lent.

As the pastor, I laid down just one rule, which might seem like a silly rule unless you attend a mainline church yourself: Lenten reflections must not be godless.

No Godless Testimonies

In *After Virtue*, Alasdair MacIntyre says that "a practice involves standards of excellence and obedience to rules as well as achievement of goods. To enter into a practice is to accept the authority of those standards and inadequacy of my own performance as judged by them."[1] If this were to be a Christian practice, our testimony was accountable to the tradition of Christian testimony itself. What could we testify to on Sunday morning that we could not just as easily testify to on National Public Radio?

So as a minister and teacher of Christian practices, I didn't want Lenten reflections limited to subjects like "All the good that civic-minded people can accomplish when they work together," or "Why New Haven needs a stronger living wage ordinance," or "What I have learned about myself in psychotherapy." But as long as God was in them, those things could be too.

Trusting that God would be in this, I tried to keep myself, as the pastor, out of it. When members offered to show me their reflections beforehand, I told them that I trusted them and would prefer to hear them on the same Sunday as the rest of the congregation.

What follows are some of the testimonies themselves, with my own reflections about the practices they embody. You see, what I learned as a pastor is that the *practice of testimony* turned out to be *testimony about practices*.

Without using the traditional words, these Christians were reflecting on where they had seen God. From what I heard in their words, in each case, it was the practices of the faith that had opened their eyes.

The first testimony came from our moderator, the chief lay leader of the congregation, who has always been in leadership during my five years here and long before that. David is in his early fifties, an architect with close-cropped hair and a reserved New England manner. I had assumed he was going to speak about a recent long-range planning leadership meeting, but instead he spoke about another retreat that had taken place four years earlier.

David

I grew up in an agnostic household where Lent was an exotic part of other people's lives, but I'd like to relate a time in my life, much longer than forty days, when I was in a kind of spiritual wilderness, cut off from connections between my true self and the people around me.

In 1983, at the age of thirty-four, I came out as a gay man, first to myself, then to my family and friends. Loyalties were stretched, some toppled, most survived. I divorced my wife and struggled to find what it meant to be a gay father to our five-year-old daughter.

I was in church every week, singing in the choir but not a member of the church, participating in but not connected to worship. I served on the missions committee, and when I was invited to serve on a search committee for an interim minister, I figured it would be a good time to join the church, but I was still in the wilderness.

One Sunday afternoon in August 1997 I was back in my office, working alone against a long-term deadline. There was a church leadership meeting at Lillian's home at 5:00, and for reasons I don't understand, I decided to go.

It was hot. I didn't feel comfortable with the people there. I didn't know what would happen. We started with a simple exercise: Lillian read a passage of Scripture about the transforming power of the Holy Spirit. Good stuff. Then she asked each of us to write about a transformation in our own lives.

I couldn't think of a "safe" example, so I wrote about the personal transformation I experienced in coming out, in accepting myself as a gay man. No one had to know: I was writing this for myself.

But when Lillian asked if anyone wanted to share their story, the Spirit moved me to volunteer. I didn't know what would happen. There was a lump in my throat and my palms were sweaty. I took a leap of faith. It was a leap back from the wilderness into a new relationship with God, one based on my true nature. It didn't hurt that no one gasped or avoided me: in fact I felt affirmation. In moving me to speak from my heart, the Spirit had also transformed my relationship with the congregation.

I felt radiant, lighter than air. I felt that I had found home.
I hope we can learn together how to call others from the
wilderness to a home in this church.

The Practice of Hospitality

After David offered his reflection, he rejoined the choir to sing the
offertory anthem red-faced. There were people in tears, as there would
be every Sunday during this practice of testimony.

My sermon that day was on spiritual practices, but I could have
thrown it out and no one would have noticed. Visitors commented
to me that they loved the worship service, but on a later week I would
see visitors leave in the middle of worship, after the testimonies. Testimony would turn out to be a risky practice, and the normally pri-
vate David had raised the bar.

I was struck by what David said about the role other practices
had played in his journey. I remember the retreat he described very
well. I was a new minister, and the congregation was very small,
surviving but not thriving, and the leaders were tired. It had taken
them eighteen months to call me as their minister after some years of
conflict and a church split. Now that I was here, they wanted to
rest. Raring to go after my first few months, I called a leadership
retreat.

I'd like to say that I opened my own home as a practice of hospitality, but really I was hoping that the leaders' curiosity to see where
I lived might overcome their exhaustion. In the end, my small living
room was full and the store-bought cookies went around like the
loaves and fishes. David was not the only one to tell his story that hot
day. Looking back, hospitality as a practice played a role. Outside of
the church meeting room with its ghosts of fights past, God did a
new thing in someone's living room.

David had been a participant in the church long before that retreat four years ago. It was the practice of singing that had drawn
him to the church and kept him there. As a musician, he had found
his place in the choir and had been shaped by it even before he considered himself fully engaged.

David said in his reflection, "I was in church every week, singing in the choir but not a member of the church, participating in but not connected to worship." Perhaps through the Christian practice of singing, God had been participating with David all along, laying the groundwork for his later testimony, the practice that would result in his deeper involvement with the church.

Still, there was no question, as David described it in his reflection, that the welcome he felt that day in 1997 was a new hospitality, a welcoming of him just as he was. People had known David was gay before that day, but he had not spoken about it publicly with the church. The congregation didn't change that day; David did, by offering his testimony. But then his testimony changed the community who heard it, as it changed us again in worship when he told the story four years later.

Testimony seems to have no beginning or end, no alpha or omega. After we tell God's story, it tells us, and then we have a new story to tell. The stories shape the community, and the community returns with new stories. But both the telling and the hearing have the power to transform.

The hospitality of that day ended up becoming a theme of growth for our small congregation. Before we grew numerically, we grew spiritually in this practice. After decades of being known by some people as a cold church, we started eating together more often, welcoming one another, listening to one another. The people who joined appreciated this hospitality and practiced it after they arrived. Today we are known as a welcoming church.

Every church would say they believe in hospitality. They just don't practice it. It's the practice that makes transformation possible. But what allows us to start practicing what we preach? And what prevents us from doing it?

Dorothy Bass and Craig Dykstra relate a lack of hospitality to fear.[2] I found this insight very helpful as I reflected on my own congregation's ups and downs in the area of hospitality. What we first recognized in theory required practice. As I look at our history of hospitality as a congregation, I can see that our hospitality has increased as our fear decreased.

My hope for the Lenten reflections was that in watching a few people offer testimony, we all would feel less fearful testifying in our everyday lives. Perhaps what happened for us in practicing hospitality could happen for us in sharing our faith.

Another week, we heard from John, a husband and a father of two boys. John married into a family in which his in-laws were active church members, but by the time I arrived as minister, that younger generation and their children were entirely absent from our church life. John told how he joined the church and also discussed some of the practices he engaged in as he discovered the liturgical seasons of the church year.

John, a math teacher with a passion for sports, who looks like a disheveled Hollywood actor, usually wears jeans and sweatshirts. But on this Sunday when he delivered the Lenten reflection, he wore a suit.

John

This Lenten reflection is about the current forty days and nights and the Advent season before last Christmas.

If you remember, there was a study finding that America's youth were overweight because they were watching TV and drinking soda. (Don't tell my son I said this; he'd be mortified.) Really that article spoke to me, so I decided to give up TV and Coca Cola for Lent. If you know me, these are no small temptations, especially during the NCAA college basketball championships, March Madness.

It turns out it's not so difficult for me to say no to these things, but to face how I use my time or how I sometimes waste it. I'm a teacher, and I bring my work home with me. I coach at school, I recycle most nights at school, I take Johnny to hockey practices and games, I go to meetings. Like most of you, the list is endless.

As many of you know, my younger son, Drew, is low-functioning autistic. Since his diagnosis five years ago, my wife and I have spent a lot of time taking turns, one of us trying to do things with Drew, the other doing other things that need to be done in our lives. If anything, you can see how precious time should be.

What I have pieced together about myself over the last few years is that the mindless clicking on of the TV and trips to the fridge, or many other devices I have found to escape my reality, stem from a helplessness that I grew up with—with alcoholism and divorce in my family—and that I ironically feel now, in not being able to help Drew express himself. In some crazy way, I have dealt with the guilt and frustration by turning it on myself, with late hours and the disappointment of not being able to do some of the basic things I need to do each day with my time.

So when Lillian gave the sermon during last Advent about being on God's time and handed out the purple ribbons, that had a profound effect on me. (I'm still wearing it.) It is a slow process, but there are more times each day when I think of God. I had always thought faith would push itself through no matter what you were doing with your time (mind and body). God is all powerful, but you must meet him halfway. You must practice your faith, not try to fit it in around other things in your schedule. So I spend more time with Drew on his terms instead of trying to fix him. He's probably on God's time more than most of us. Let him fix me.

A couple of weeks ago, Lillian talked about how powerful it would be if we all prayed twice a day. Since this Lent season has begun, I have tried to think of God the last thing before I sleep and the first thing when I wake. I pray a lot more, although it needs work. And you know what? Without some of the late hours of caffeine and video images, I have started remembering my dreams again and writing them in my prayer journal that I got on one church retreat. I consider my dreams a form of prayer and one of the Holy Spirit's ways of guiding me. Again it is a slow process, but I am very grateful to this church for helping me forgive myself and see my time through more faithful eyes.

Keeping the Sabbath

John was the last person I expected to give a testimony on the practices of the faith. I didn't think he'd have time to engage in these things. I think that ministers often set the bar too low. John, one of the busiest people in the congregation with some of the most difficult claims on his time, was the perfect person to lay out practices that help us value time.

Time seems to me to be the second most urgent pastoral crisis after money, and the two are intertwined as the most common reasons we give for not being what God wants us to be. Baseball practices and low bank account balances are ironic excuses for avoiding the practices that might relieve some of the pressure.

John could epitomize the frenzy, but in his Lenten reflection he was a pilgrim on a journey toward deeper understanding. While there are chunks of time during baseball season when we do not see him or his son Johnny at church, and while John never mentioned the word "Sunday," the practice he was describing was about honoring time, and that takes us into the practice of Sabbath keeping.

Dorothy Bass lays out the promise of this practice: "Whether we know the term *Sabbath* or not, we the harried citizens of late modernity yearn for the reality. We need Sabbath even though we doubt we have time for it. As the new century dawns, the practice of Sabbath keeping may be a gift just waiting to be unwrapped, a confirmation that we are not without help in shaping the renewing ways of life for which we long."[3]

People are hungering for wisdom on the subject of time. Sabbath is not the only unwrapped gift we have waiting for us in the Christian tradition. The liturgical seasons are also there to remind us that God's calendar is more nuanced and graceful than we imagine as we rush from one appointment to the next. Just the fact that the church introduces a *different* calendar raises the provocative question of who invents time.

During Advent I spent three weeks preaching on the subject of valuing time as an unearned gift from God. At the beginning of the season, we handed out small purple ribbons and asked people to tie them to their watches or their date books. The ribbons were to remind us that in Advent, time is revealed as an illusion so much smaller than God. In Advent, Old Testament prophets predict a future birth that we in the present know has already happened. Advent is all about unraveling time and reminding us that in its mystery, time belongs not to us but to God.

I had wondered if people would wear the ribbons. As a minister I had thought that the ribbons would be a less severe conversation starter than ashes on one's forehead at the beginning of Lent, but I wanted conversations to start nonetheless. Looking back, I was trying for testimony again and at the same time wondering if the possibility of being asked to testify would turn people away from the practice.

What happened surprised me. Not only did people wear the ribbons, but after Advent ended, they refused to take them off. By the time John delivered the Lenten reflection, John's ribbon on his watch was ragged. The prayer journal that he had started at a retreat over a year ago was a tool I had forgotten about but one that he had held on to. In Lent when I asked people to pray twice daily, I also sent them home with a bookmark that laid out morning and evening prayers. Some people needed no such guidelines, but I knew that others might need something to hold in their hands.

Through John's testimony I was reminded that for some people concrete objects play an important role in Christian practice. John, a math teacher and an athlete, cares about the physical world so passionately that he spends his free time recycling paper, cardboard, cans, and bottles in all the communities he is a part of. Things matter. As ministers we may forget about people like John. We may forget to link ideas to things that people can touch and hold and see.

Furthermore, when it comes to practices around time, the secular world is all too ready to provide things—handheld tools that promise order. The Franklin Planner offers the illusion that we can plan anything. The Palm Pilot even offers us the ability to steer time itself, as a pilot. When it comes to time, God has slipped from the dubious position of being my copilot to being a passenger on a busy schedule I am supposed to be piloting.

An ad for the *Christian Century* magazine shows an entry on a Palm Pilot that reads "Check out *Christian Century*." Later in the day we might check out God, before we go to the gym and after we attend a time management seminar.

Tools around time abound in the world, but they don't solve the problems or end the pain. The Christian tradition offers practices and symbols, but sometimes God just breaks in with a disruption in the schedule that makes us see time in a new way.

That is what my husband ended up describing when he offered the Lenten reflection on the fourth Sunday. My travel schedule ended up pulling him into a hospital visit, which drew him into the practices of caring for the sick, honoring the elders of the church, and sharing some thoughts about living and dying well.

Lou

Good morning, brothers and sisters. This morning I would like to talk about the spiritual guidance I have received from older men, and in particular one man in this church, the Reverend Ed Edmonds, who many of us call "Doc."

The relationships between fathers and sons can be very tricky. So many layers of meanings—anger, pride, rebellion, grief, pity, humiliation—the love of fathers and sons can be confusing. I think that is why it's a good idea to have grandfathers.

Both of my grandfathers were wonderful, generous men. Flawed, I'm sure, but since I knew them only when I was a child, I still hold them in dreamlike perfection in my mind's eye. Anyway, I suspect I've been hunting surrogate grandfathers my whole life. I'm interested in how men can age with grace, courage, even elegance.

A few months ago, Newt Schenck ended up in the hospital. As most of you know, Newt is a pillar of New Haven, a remarkable civic leader, and a sporadic attendee of Sunday services here at the Church of the Redeemer. Lillian was traveling out of town, so I swung by Newt's room at Yale–New Haven Hospital, where I am working to organize a union. There was a sign on Newt's door that said that he was tired and to check with his nurse to see if he would take visitors. He agreed to see me, so I went in. He said, "How nice of you to come by. What can I do for you?"

I told him that the hospital police had been chasing me down the hall, and was it okay for me to hide in his room?

We laughed a bit and then settled down to a long, lively conversation. Matters local and international, the future of New Haven (a city we both love), the great attributes and great flaws of our mutual alma mater (Yale), the hopes and perils of the biotechnology industry, the history of the labor movement—we talked and talked. I had to tear myself out of the room. I felt that God had given me a gift that day.

Shortly after that I resumed reading for an hour or so each week to Doctor Edmonds, who sits here most Sundays as our own rather elegant prophet. Visually impaired since he was a young man, Doctor Edmonds has a brilliant mind. But even more, he has a lion's heart.

Doc is a nationally known civil rights leader. He had his life threatened during the fifties and sixties. He built a black middle class in New Haven. The stories are endless. The clearest picture that I have of Doc is from the winter of 1995–96. Yale was trying to significantly weaken and perhaps destroy our unions at the university. We had endured two month-long strikes. Three hundred people—union leaders, community activists, and a few clergy—committed civil disobedience on Grove Street in the middle of campus and refused to clear the intersection. When the police reached Doc, they refused to arrest him. I remember Doc fighting, really angry, demanding to be taken down to the jail and processed with the other protesters.

In short, I am a student of Doc. I have watched Doc, and I have learned. I have learned about life and I have learned about God. Here is what I have learned about life:

Read, read, and keep reading.

Raise strong daughters.

Temper your anger with humor, but stay angry.

Paint your dreams with large brushstrokes.

Have strong opinions.

Spend time with younger people even when you feel horrible. And as your health wanes and the tethers that hold you to this earth get looser and looser, realize that from your new height you have an even bigger vision to share with those still tied to the ground.

Here is what I have learned about the liberator God that Doc and I both worship.

God challenges us to engage in struggle.

God asks us to sacrifice.

God asks us to carry heavy burdens.

God sacrificed God's only Son to redeem our broken world, and compared to that pain and sacrifice, we don't have to do very much.

Just fight for God's kingdom of justice and peace.

I pray for myself and the other young men of this church that as we age we can follow in the footsteps of the old lions— fighting for what we believe in, giving strength to those around us, and pointing the way to God's kingdom on earth.

Healing

The practices of our faith give our lives shape and meaning. We need that when things get complicated. Sometimes we need to see other people's practices in order to unearth our own.

Lou, at the age of thirty-four, was trying to understand what that life-giving way of life looks like by turning to older men in the congregation for spiritual guidance. In the practice of testimony that day, he talked about what these men had taught him about God, and about that life-giving way of life. But none of this would have happened outside of the practice of healing and the basic Christian practice of visiting the sick when they cannot come to the church.

Lou's visit to the hospital reminded him of another lapsed practice, that of visiting and reading to Doc at his home. Practices seem to feed into one another. One practice reminds us to try another. At the heart of this Lenten reflection was healing, not just the healing of people's bodies, not just the healing of the spirit that comes from being honored and listened to, but wholeness. As Lou laid out his own search for grandfathers, it was clear that he was searching for healing in his own life, not in the sense of seeking cure, but of seeking wholeness.

Lou and the men he spoke about all believe in a healing that encompasses the whole community. A civic leader, a civil rights activist, a union organizer—none of the three men was passively waiting for that healing. At different stages in their lives, all three believe that wholeness comes in the struggle, and that can be a healing not just of a body but of the nations.

And so it seems natural that conversations about the state of the city and the fate of the labor movement would take place in a tangle of IV tubes and heart monitors in a hospital room. In the practice of healing, we pray that the community will be healed and that we will be whole.

On the other hand, as Lou, a healthy marathon runner and father of young children looks at Newt and Doc, he must confront the betrayal of their human bodies and the inevitable betrayal of his own. What healing practice can unravel Crohn's disease or Parkinson's disease when it takes two old lions and knocks them down with pain? For Lou, part of the practice of healing is understanding their lives, listening to their stories, and then telling those stories to others. Their testimony becomes his testimony as he describes a God who is both his God and Doc's God.

We long for the understanding that we, in these scarred and personal bodies, have mattered to God and will matter as we go into the practice of dying well. When Lou talked about the lessons he learned, he said, "Spend time with younger people even when you feel horrible. And as your health wanes and the tethers that hold you to this earth get looser and looser, realize that from your new height you have an even bigger vision to share with those still tied to the ground." We don't talk about these things very often in the presence of those who may be going through them.

In society we do not talk about "tethers to the earth getting looser" but only about "getting better." Nevertheless, Lou had spoken with the men about this subject of failing bodies, and their words had mattered to him. Doc was in church to hear Lou's testimony. His Parkinson's changes him day to day, and this was the first time the congregation had seen Doc in a wheelchair. There was an urgency in Lou's testimony that made us all uncomfortable but also relieved that someone was telling these men what we all wanted to say. Their leadership as well as their illnesses mattered to us all.

In healing and caring for those whose bodies grow weak, we have to look at mortality and how it affects the wholeness of us all. As people of faith we can aspire to more than dying. We can aspire to practice our faith into the next stage of eternity and, as we approach it, to die well.

In Lou's testimony he was noticing the divine ground underneath both illness and health, underneath the times of fatherhood and grandfatherhood, underneath running a marathon or whatever the next race is that God lays before us. Lou could not have done any of this alone; it could only happen when two or three were gathered in Christ's name, and somebody decided to talk about it.

A Voice from the Past

As our church grew in the practice of testimony, we realized that we were playing out our Puritan history, from the days when new church members had to stand up and offer a conversion narrative to the church. I discovered other testimonies from my own Congregationalist history that were against one theological position or another, or took on the larger issues of society, from abolition to card playing.

But many were full of the very same longing, faith, and mystery that I experience in the twenty-first century.

And sometimes a testimony was recorded in history that sounds so much like one from a Congregational church today that I am stunned. Even while I cannot imagine what exactly it was like to be there, in that different time, I find myself aware of the Holy Spirit's presence when I read words like the following, from Anne Wilcox of Stockbridge, Massachusetts, in the 1830s.

> I shall now attempt to describe my feelings. They was first wrought upon, when I was absent from this place. I think the first cause derived, from my hearing of the revival in Stockbridge. I soon felt dejected, & unworthy to be here in such an interesting time. But still I was anxious to return, & to come home with a strong determination to obtain an interest in the Saviour if possible. I felt as if then was the <accepted> time, if ever. & I trust it was. The first meeting I attended after my return here, was with a heavy heart, & ready to break with anguish under a sense of my situation. The Lord saw fit to strive with me, 2 or 3 weeks, before he made me willing to submit wholly to his will. In that time, I attempted often to Pray, but when I returned to my room it was with a heart as heavy as when entered. I was anxious to read the Bible, & found many verry precious promises for those that would seek the Lord diligently. Which encouraged me still to go on, but I found that I was entirely dependent & that I must throw myself upon the hands of a just & offended God & that I could do nothing but to plead guilty abandoned [illegible deletion] creature. I think I can say from that time I obtained much relief in my mind, & much comfort in Prayer, & in reading the Bible, I found it to be quite a new book to me. & my sincere Prayer is that I may ever continue in the same, & may it be of others for me.[4]

From almost two hundred years ago, I can hear in this woman's testimony a similar message to those that I have heard over the last years in my church—a story of a person lost, dejected, and then by God's grace finding meaning.

Growing in the Practices of Faith

In *After Virtue*, Alasdair MacIntyre tells us that throwing a football pass is not a practice, but that the game of football is. "Every practice requires a certain kind of relationship between those who participate in it."[5] Testimony goes so much deeper than an individual's deep thoughts. Other players are involved in a game, the rules of which we cannot simply make up as we go along yet which may change as the playing community sees fit.

For the Church of the Redeemer, that first season of Lenten reflections led to many years of testimony in all seasons and styles. Testimony shaped that church as surely as it shaped me as a minister.

Now I find myself far from New England, serving another church in the suburbs of Chicago, but I am never far from the practice that shaped us all. I continue to hear about testimonies back at Redeemer, just as the testimonies of the Puritans call out from the past. And as the First Congregational Church of Glen Ellyn tries out this new practice, we open our ears for the testimonies of the future. May we all continue to tell God's story in our own words.

That's my testimony.

Notes

1. Alasdair MacIntyre, *After Virtue*, 2nd ed. (Notre Dame, IN: Univ. of Notre Dame Press, 1984), 190.
2. Dorothy Bass, ed., *Practicing Our Faith: A Way of Life for Searching People*, Jossey-Bass Practicing Our Faith Series (San Francisco: Jossey-Bass, 1998), 31–32.
3. Ibid., 76.
4. Ann Wilcox, Stockbridge "Experiences," c. 1830–33, Stockbridge Library Association, Historical Collection. The author would like to thank Ken Minkema of Yale University for bringing this source to her attention.
5. MacIntyre, *After Virtue*, 191.

TAKING RISKS

Full Gospel Church

Scott A. Benhase
St. Philip's Episcopal Church
Durham, North Carolina

> *St. Philip's Episcopal Church sits on a city block in the
> economically challenged center of Durham, North Carolina. As a
> diverse urban congregation, St. Philip's has had to be very
> intentional about discerning its identity and mission. As the
> church's rector, Scott Benhase, shares in this essay, that process of
> discernment has required both generosity of spirit and courage—
> but when St. Philip's took a risk that it sensed God calling it to
> take, it found itself transformed.*

In many ways leadership is the capacity to disappoint people at a
level they can manage. The opposite is equally true: it is the capacity
to bring people along at a pace they can accept without excessive
stress or chaos. Ronald A. Heifetz and Marty Linsky refer to this as
the leader raising and lowering the temperature in a particular context.[1] Turning up the heat gets people excited, alert, and ready for
action (either in support or in opposition). If this heat lasts too long,
people will burn up. Lowering the heat creates time and space for
people to absorb what is happening. Sometimes leaders have their
hand on the thermostat. At other times they cannot control the temperature at all. I have often found myself in both situations.

Jesus spent a lot of time with his hand on the thermostat. He was usually turning up the heat on the scribes and Pharisees, and sometimes on his disciples. He also knew when he needed to get away, not so much to lower the temperature, but rather to keep from burning himself up (and the people around him) before it was God's *kairos*.

Leading a diverse urban congregation requires a particular capacity for leadership and a steady hand on the thermostat. In the diversity of the city, an urban congregation is likely to attract all sorts and conditions of people. Leading such a group of people and inviting them into a deeper sense of discipleship demands a leader with a reasonably thick skin and the ability to enjoy all temperature levels.

St. Philip's Church is a downtown congregation on East Main Street in Durham, North Carolina. We own almost our entire city block. On our block we have the church nave and sanctuary; a parish house where administrative and formation ministries take place; a parish hall, which serves both parish and community functions; a large cloister garden, which includes a columbarium, outdoor sanctuary (complete with altar and font), and prayer labyrinth; and the Urban Ministries Center and its two buildings used to house its community kitchen, homeless shelter, food and clothing pantry, addiction recovery services, and administrative offices. St. Philip's Church has a membership of about 355 households representing more than 700 baptized members. Our members come from all over the metropolitan area, though the vast majority are from the city of Durham.

Our understanding of our mission and ministry comes out of the discernment of our context. Our parish mission statement reads:

> St. Philip's is a holy place where we worship God. Our worship forms us into a community of Christians. By prayer, sacrament, and fellowship, we nourish and sustain one another in our individual lives and ministries. We obey the Gospel call to bring the light of hope in Jesus Christ to all people. We offer welcome, support, food, and shelter to all in need without pride, prejudice, or judgment. We have responsibility to the entire Durham community, especially our downtown neighborhood.

What we are attempting to do at St. Philip's Church is to have it all, that is, quality and quantity, spiritual and numerical growth, reaching in and reaching out to all people across lines of race, gender, and sexual orientation. All of this, of course, is greatly affected by our location downtown, surrounded as we are by the Departments of Mental and Public Health, public housing, and local government.

St. Philip's is a theologically diverse parish. We often joke that where two or three St. Philippians are gathered, you will find four or five theological positions. Rather than insist on uniformity or theological correctness, we seek to break through the tyranny of the liberal/conservative polarities of the church. Church liberals and church conservatives seem to be two sides of the same doctrinal coin. They both believe that if they just beat on the church's doctrine long enough everyone will come to see the rightness of their position. At St. Philip's we seek a different way of being the church.

Early on in my ministry I can remember preaching entire sermons aimed at people who disagreed with me. I went to great pains to find the right scripture to justify myself. But over the years I have learned how to love those people and, I believe, some of them have come to love me even though we still disagree. We came to love, respect, and trust one another, and that made the difference. The development of mutual trust along with a confidence in God's power and the truth of the gospel allows for diversity to be an asset and not a liability. It is not the theological aptitude, the location of the building, or even the size of the population that determines a vibrant ministry. Those are all factors, but they are not determining factors. Growing into such diversity requires being open to new people, new ideas, new worship patterns, and new power arrangements. Without mutual trust and confidence in God, such diversity will overwhelm everyone.

We like to refer to ourselves as a "full gospel church," which is a term borrowed from fundamentalism that we have reworked for our own use. For too long mainstream Christianity has allowed fundamentalists to define what it means to follow Jesus. It takes no real effort to say that one believes this or that about Jesus. There is no real cost in that. What really matters is that a people live the faith as disciples of Jesus. So we try to remind ourselves regularly of what Jesus says a disciple looks like and acts like so that we can continue to learn to live that way ourselves.

To be a full gospel church we must not only proclaim salvation in Jesus, but we must also practice forgiveness, serve the poor, and love our enemies. To be full gospel Christians, we must take seriously the call to proclaim the good news of God in Christ. And, with equal seriousness, we must respond to our Lord's call to find him in the poor, the outcast, and those who have lost hope.

Christian churches often live out only one half of the gospel. Either they see the sum total of their discipleship as proclaiming the gospel with words, or they are reluctant to talk about the good news at all and prefer only to let their deeds speak for them. Neither way is more faithful. The problem comes when we do not see the necessity and completeness that calls us to the full gospel. On the one side, the church can become, as my grandfather used to say, all bark and no tree. The church can bark out the good news, telling people to repent and believe in the gospel. But if that is all the church does, we can find ourselves drifting into triumphalism. The other side is equally as dangerous for disciples. Being a servant to the poor and to the hopeless can lead to despair because we will quickly learn that poverty will never go away this side of heaven, and hope can be crushed in a violent world.

To be complete disciples, we need to embrace and live out the full gospel. The full gospel of Jesus will keep us humble and always hopeful even when all signs indicate otherwise. Our service to the poor will humbly check an urge to be triumphant in our proclamation of the gospel. And our proclamation of the gospel will always remind us that by serving the poor, the sick, and the prisoner, we are all held securely in the loving arms of Jesus. Embracing and incarnating the full gospel of Jesus in our lives keeps us from both prideful triumphalism and existential despair.

The full gospel of Jesus will be countercultural in our secular culture and sometimes even in the church. Living out the full gospel of Jesus will get us in trouble with both liberals and conservatives. At other times we will find common cause with them. Sometimes we will need to stand against the secular culture, and at other times we will find that we can work effectively with people outside the church. Being full gospel Christians means that we will never be completely at home in this world.

Therefore, the particular challenges facing St. Philip's Church are not unique to our context. They are challenges that are facing the church throughout contemporary Western culture. How then can we continue to live in this tension of unity in diversity? How can we continue to grow numerically when newcomers can, at first, experience our diversity as not standing for anything other than being diverse? Our incorporation process offers one answer. Newcomers through our seekers and catechumenate classes learn that we do hold and proclaim orthodox Christian teaching. Some are often surprised to discover this. Another answer is the preaching of the clergy. Our preaching continues to help shape and define the understanding of our community as peculiarly Christian. All three clergy strive to offer solid preaching based on the *via positiva*. In other words, in our preaching we try to proclaim positively who we are and who we are becoming rather than defining ourselves by who we are not. This then shapes the parish culture and helps people give themselves greater permission to become such a community of disciples.

We have a reputation in our community for outreach. But that outreach can be done only because there is a congregation who has recognized the claims of Jesus on their lives and who has sought to make manifest those claims in our neighborhood. Thus, outreach is merely inreach turned outward. The congregation must be fed if they are going to feed anyone else.

We have developed the counterintuitive insight that faithful urban ministry begins with ministry to our own children. The strongest aspect of our ministry right now is our ministry to and with our own children. We have developed the habit of discipling our own children. And because we do that well, people will drive from the suburbs, past other churches, to come to St. Philip's. We have children from two-parent families, children from single-parent families, adopted children, and children of gay- and lesbian-parent families. It might be overly simplistic to say that the key to urban parish ministry begins with ministry to and with children, but we do not think so. We do not neglect adult discipling, our music ministry, our varied worship, our commitment to serve Jesus in the poor and lost of our downtown community, or any other aspect of what it means to be church. We take all those aspects of our common life with the utmost seriousness and energy. But we do believe that the key is to begin with Christian formation of children.

St. Philip's was founded in 1878 when Deacon Joseph Cheshire responded to a request from some Episcopalians in Durham to hold services in the growing tobacco town. Deacon Cheshire walked from nearby Chapel Hill to Durham to hold the first services. The congregation was named after Philip the Deacon in honor of Deacon Cheshire. St. Philip's grew as Durham grew. Throughout the early half of the twentieth century, Durham was a center of both tobacco and textiles. The parish roll reflected Durham's character in that many of the professional class of Durham were members.

After World War II Durham continued its growth in these two industries while the suburban areas around the city expanded. By the 1960s urban renewal was under way in downtown Durham. Stores closed or moved to the suburbs. Also, many of the homes that were nearby the church were either razed or converted into businesses. A downtown loop was constructed to allow motorists to bypass downtown. All these factors impacted St. Philip's ability to attract new members.

Also in the 1960s the civil rights movement reached Durham. The parish had never really engaged the issue before. The rector at this time struggled to lead the parish through this period of intense change. One event served to sabotage what progress was being made. A group of students and professors from Duke and North Carolina Central Universities began Malcolm X University in some old buildings across the street from St. Philip's. It received start-up funds from a variety of sources, one of which was a grant from the national Episcopal Church. When parishioners learned of this, many were angry at the national church. Some of the anger was due to the fact that they were not consulted, but most of it was a result of their opposition to integration and the changing race relations in our country. This was a profound trauma to the congregation. People withheld their pledges in protest of the national church's actions. The parish weathered this storm but was greatly weakened by it just in time for other divisive issues like the ordination of women and a revision of the Book of Common Prayer.

By the late 1970s the rector who had led the parish through the civil rights struggle, women's ordination, and the new prayer book was exhausted. He resigned to take a position as a social worker in the community but soon after died suddenly. His death divided the parish. Some claimed that the parish's divisiveness had literally killed him while others denied any connection between his death and the parish's conflict. In the midst of this came my predecessor who had a strong vision for St. Philip's as a center for urban ministry in the city. His style was not one of consensus building. He used his considerable gifts of charm and passion to move the congregation toward a greater witness in downtown. While some resisted these efforts, many were enamored with the rector's vision. Under his tenure, the parish began the Community Kitchen, a jail ministry, and St. Philip's House. Along with ecumenical partners, he led the construction of the Urban Ministries Center on vacant parish property. This became a place for various ecumenical ministries to offer their services, including St. Philip's Community Kitchen. By the early 1990s the parish had reached some stability, but most people still regarded downtown Durham as a dangerous place to be.

When I arrived in the summer of 1995, the parish seemed anxious and divided. The interim rector had died of cancer. Because of his illness, much of what an interim was supposed to have done had in fact not been done. The parish had not done its work during the interim since much of their emotional and spiritual focus was on ministering to a dying priest. I sensed right away that I was going to have to complete the work of the interim rector. I also concluded that it may result in a short tenure for me. Helping the parish through the transition would require me to function differently than if I expected a long tenure. There was a division among parishioners over the parish's focus. Some were committed to the parish's urban outreach and did not feel we needed to focus on ministering to one another. Others felt that all the focus over the previous fifteen years had been on outreach to the detriment of our caring for one another.

I tried from the outset to name the false dichotomy that had been created. There was no reason why the parish could not have both a vibrant ministry in the community and an equally vibrant ministry to one another. To do both of these, I knew we had to build confidence and trust in one another and in my leadership. We brought in a consultant and developed a twelve-point action plan that we estimated would take about seven years to complete. The plan was multifaceted, but the cornerstone was a master planning process leading to a major renovation and expansion of our facilities. This was a big risk. Failing to follow through and complete the plan would have a profoundly harmful effect on the parish's life. By 2000 we had completed all twelve points of the plan two years earlier than expected. The other parts of the twelve-point plan focused primarily on adult and children's Christian formation and the development of pastoral and fellowship ministries in the parish. Weathering the changes of the first few years was difficult for everyone in the parish. I discovered in the process how important trust development is in parish ministry and how leadership that is both strong and flexible is crucial for healthy development.

Recently our convictions about the nature of our particular Christian community were tested. In September 2003 our bishop announced he would allow a pastoral rite blessing same sex couples in our diocese. I approached St. Philip's vestry with this news. I told the vestry that since we have many gay and lesbian persons in the parish, they would soon learn of the bishop's decision and approach me to find out what our parish was going to do. Rather than being reactive to this, I asked the vestry to be proactive. To do nothing or to pretend that this issue would simply go away would not be honest, and we would not be true to our calling as leaders of the parish. I suggested that we as rector and vestry enter into a period of conversation and discernment around this issue with the following ground rules: (1) unless consensus was reached, no decision would be made; (2) there would be no time limit on our discernment; (3) if consensus was reached, then it would be honored by all vestry persons (in order to avoid dissension and possible sabotage); and (4) our discernment would be confidential so we could discern our calling free of outside pressure. The vestry agreed to enter into discernment under those ground rules, and we began to do so that night at the September vestry meeting.

The vestry ended up devoting five months to a discussion and exploration of this issue. Over the months of discussion, some expressed discomfort about having any kind of liturgical rite, while others felt quite comfortable from the beginning that this was what the parish should do. Some felt that if we were going to have a rite, then it ought to look much like the marriage liturgy in the Book of Common Prayer. Others disagreed and held that it should only be a blessing and have no sacramental quality to it. After much prayer, listening, and conversation, consensus was reached that we should have a blessing rite for same sex couples.

Once we reached consensus we still recognized that our consensus did not mean that everyone was now in the same place on this issue. What we sought to do in finding consensus was to honor the diversity of theological positions we represented while also responding to the current reality of where the Episcopal Church was corporately. We also recognized that our consensus as a vestry should not be mistaken for certainty. Like all discernment of God's will, we recognized in humility that we are not God and could not know for sure what God would have us do. But that should not paralyze us into inaction. Historical circumstances brought us to this place. We all felt strongly that God is sovereign and Jesus is Lord. If we were in error in this decision, then God would correct us in God's time. If our consensus was in accordance with God's purposes, then God would bless our life together.

The vestry announced its consensus position at our annual meeting in January 2004. We also announced this as the beginning of a time of listening and discernment among all members of the church—a period of discussing, praying, and reflecting on what God would have us do. During this congregational process the parish clergy were open about their thoughts and feelings on the matter and encouraged the laity to speak with them and others about how they felt. We set aside five Sundays in February as well as a portion of our parish retreat in March for open conversation and dialogue. These scheduled conversations were widely attended and had some basic ground rules. Participants were asked to share their thoughts without denigrating other participants' positions. If we were truly going to listen to one another and hear what God was saying to us in our conversation, then we had to have an a priori respect for one another's words.

What we learned as a result of this process was that as a parish we were not of one mind on this issue. Some were concerned that blessing same sex unions would deviate from the teachings and traditions of the church. Some also felt that the proposed rite, because it was not sacramental, fell short of the acknowledgment and support they believed the Christian community should offer gay and lesbian Christians. But we also learned that while we were of divided minds, we remained of one Spirit. There was no stronger evidence of this truth than the process in which we engaged. We created a spiritual space where all members of our Christian community had a safe, secure, and supportive environment to speak their understanding of how Jesus was calling us. Our common discernment resulted in our seeing each other with new eyes, hearing and celebrating the diverse voices present in our parish. It was also a testimony to our embodiment of Jesus' command to love one another as he loves us (John 15:12).

At our mid-year congregational meeting that June, we offered another opportunity for those gathered to speak to this issue. The vestry made it clear that they wanted to hear from everybody before coming to a decision. Very little was said. The parish was ready. Two weeks later the vestry decided unanimously that it was time for us to move forward with the blessing of same sex unions. They passed a resolution encouraging the rector to provide this pastoral rite to members of the parish. The process in which we engaged put to the test our claims about having unity in our diversity. The end result of nine months of discernment showed that we had actually become stronger because of, and not in spite of, our discernment on this divisive issue. We learned that we can take risks together if we are determined to love one another as Jesus loves us.

My role as the senior ordained leader in the parish is to maintain a high level of trust so that I can foster an attitude of agape love throughout the church community. Sometimes when the chaos becomes acute, it is necessary for me to insist on this love. Over time and as trust has developed, the insisting happens rarely. A community that is determined to love one another in its diversity defines that community as peculiarly Christian. Our determination to love one another defines us as much as the eucharist we celebrate together each Sunday. Our shared experience of the love of Jesus unzips our spiritual straitjackets. From my reading of the gospel, Jesus lays down only one criterion for discipleship—and it isn't theological correctness. Rather, it is the capacity to love one another as he loves us, which means to love one another all the way to the cross if need be. I don't think that on judgment day we will be asked how correct we were in our theological positions. I feel we are more likely to be asked to show God what we took on and lived out in our lives for the love of Jesus. We are working hard to remind ourselves of that every day at St. Philip's.

Notes

1. Ronald A. Heifitz and Marty Linsky, *Leadership on the Line: Staying Alive through the Dangers of Leading* (Cambridge: Harvard Business School Press, 2002), 111.

Saying Yes and Saying No

The Prayer of Jabez, The Passion of the Christ, and a Tale of Two Congregations

Kenneth H. Carter Jr.
Mount Tabor and Providence United Methodist Churches
Winston-Salem and Charlotte, North Carolina

Both Mount Tabor United Methodist Church in Winston-Salem and Providence United Methodist Church in Charlotte are located in North Carolina cities where trends in popular Christianity cannot be ignored. As frustrated as many mainline Protestant pastors may be with phenomena such as The Prayer of Jabez *or* The Passion of the Christ, *there must be some response. Sharing his experiences with these movements at subsequent churches, Kenneth Carter suggests that the practice of saying no to trendy spirituality requires an already existing practice of saying yes to the deep wisdom of practices from one's tradition.*

I have served as a parish minister for approximately twenty-two years. From 1997–2003, I was senior pastor of Mount Tabor United Methodist Church in Winston-Salem, North Carolina. In 2003 I was assigned by our bishop to the Providence United Methodist Church in Charlotte, North Carolina. These years coincided with a deep exposure to the literature on practices, as I participated in a working group of pastors that met quarterly, convened by Craig Dykstra. This experience gave me a framework to reconsider my own pastoral practices

127

and a renewed appreciation for my own tradition, one that was rooted in "practical divinity."[1]

Mount Tabor Church was and is typical of many healthy United Methodist congregations in the United States. They have constructed buildings in recent years and are presently in the process of paying for them. They have added a worship service and increased the staff. They support the denomination insofar as they are aware of what is going on with it. Significant outreach occurs in the community. The congregation embodies much of what is best about United Methodism in its institutional life.

Serving as pastor of this congregation for six years, however, I was often led to ask the question, in the midst of a great deal of activity: what is distinctively Christian about Mount Tabor United Methodist Church? Sometimes people would ask about our adult Sunday school classes, of which there were several. None was particularly doctrinal in any way. We were in close proximity to two megachurches: one Pentecostal, the other conservative Baptist. Both were strong, healthy congregations, yet we knew we were not like either in most respects. We did not exclude women from clerical leadership. We did not raise our hands in worship. We did not fuse patriotism and faith.

But could we be defined by who we were not? Who were we? The answer to this question came to me, in part, from reflecting on our origins. Bishop Rueben Job offered this description of the early Methodists.

> Methodist life was marked by a deep and authentic personal piety that led to a broad and uncompromising social involvement. Methodists were known for their prayers and for their commitment to the poor and disenfranchised. This commitment resulted in persistent efforts to build houses of prayer and worship as well as consistent efforts to visit the prisons, build schools and hospitals, and work for laws which moved toward a just and peaceful social order. . . . Because they took their relationship to Jesus Christ with utmost seriousness, their life of prayer and witness was readily identified and often very contagious as many wanted to have what

Methodists appeared to have. Among these Methodist gifts were a certain knowledge about their own salvation, an at-homeness in this world and confidence in the next, a living companionship with a living Christ, and access to the power of God that could and did transform the most broken and hopeless persons into productive, joyful and faithful. Such was the power of God in the way the Methodists lived.[2]

Mount Tabor and The Prayer of Jabez

One of the great publishing phenomena of our time is a little book entitled *The Prayer of Jabez* by Bruce Wilkinson.[3] I first heard about the prayer while visiting family in another state. I had stopped in to see a friend from college who now operates a Christian bookstore. "You have to read this book! We can't keep it in the store!" he said to me enthusiastically. The title was *The Prayer of Jabez*, taken from a little-known Old Testament passage. The prayer is simple: "Oh, that You would bless me indeed, and enlarge my territory, that Your hand would be with me, and that You would keep me from evil, that I may not cause pain!" (1 Chron. 4:10 NKJV). I returned home, not having read the book (my friend had sold out of them), only to encounter three people that very week who mentioned it. I went out and bought a copy and read its ninety-two pages over lunch. It was at times inspiring and at other times convicting. When I am reading books on the spiritual life, I try not to be too analytical or critical. That is very much my nature, but I have learned that it can be a way of avoiding something God might be saying to me. Yet, in reading *The Prayer of Jabez* and in saying the words of the prayer prayerfully, I had the sense that something essential was missing from my life.

What was missing became apparent to me as I concluded a year of helping to teach the Disciple Bible Study. Disciple is a yearlong study in which an individual, within a group of twelve people, reads approximately 80 percent of the Bible. Each session includes a time for struggling with the question of how the text calls the reader toward a deeper discipleship. Disciple had been an integral practice in the Mount Tabor congregation for a number of years. As a practice it embodies what John Wesley described as "searching the Scripture." At the course's end there is a focus on relationship with God through identification of spiritual gifts. This relationship is established through covenant, remembered in the act of Holy Communion. Within the service are the following words: "I give myself completely to you, God. Assign me to my place in your creation. Let me suffer for you. Give me the work you would have me do. Give me many tasks, or have me step aside while you call others. Put me forward or humble me. Give me riches or let me live in poverty. I freely give all that I am and all that I have to you."[4]

Both Mount Tabor and Providence congregations ordinarily begin the calendar year with some form of this prayer as a part of the Sunday liturgy. These words of the covenant prayer have been a part of our devotional life for almost 250 years. With the advent of Disciple, they have been introduced to over one million Methodists meeting in small groups. In the saying of the words at the conclusion of Disciple, we realized that our spiritual birthright, as people called Methodist, is not in the prayer of Jabez. Our spiritual heritage is captured in the words of the covenant prayer. They are profoundly biblical and express a radical dependence on God and submission to God's will. They are almost a commentary on a briefer prayer of our Lord: "Not what I want. You, what do you want?" (Matt. 26:39 MESSAGE).

Reading the words of the prayer of Jabez (and Wilkinson's commentary on it) alongside the covenant prayer presents starkly contrasting visions of the Christian life:

- One is about self-fulfillment, the other self-denial.
- One is about changing God's mind, the other about submitting to God's purpose.
- One is personal, the other is corporate.
- One is in harmony with a culture of acquisition and consumption, the other is in conflict with expanding markets and egos.

I recognized, and attempted to communicate through sermons and in pastoral conversations, that two spiritual options were before us. One we could embrace, the other we might question. In our own congregation, this was the practice of "saying yes" and "saying no." While the megachurches near us formed large groups around the reading of *The Prayer of Jabez*, we chose to reflect on the covenant prayer.

I do acknowledge that, by grace, God welcomes all of our prayers. "We do not know how to pray as we ought," the apostle Paul wrote in Romans 8:26 (NRSV). God takes the inadequacies of all of our prayers—surely my own included—hears our true intentions, and responds.

Mount Tabor and Providence churches offer approximately six to seven Disciple courses each year. Some are led by clergy, others by laity. Each has held Disciple courses over the past ten to fifteen years. For United Methodists this has led to a recovery of one of our means of grace, the searching of the Scriptures. When an individual within a small group reads the Bible daily for thirty-four weeks and is held accountable to the text and to other pilgrims, a practice begins to emerge. Craig Dykstra and Dorothy Bass have defined Christian practices as "things Christian people do together over time in response to and in light of God's active presence for the life of the world."[5] And the reading of scripture, at a deeply engaged level, creates a maturity in the congregation.

One member of Mount Tabor taught elementary school in the inner city for most of her adult life, and each day she was a sacramental presence to the children in her room. She cared about the lives of her children beyond the classroom and long after they had graduated. At times I preached about going out into the world with the compassion of Christ, knowing that, in actuality, there were those in the congregation who had been doing that long before I arrived on the scene. In effect, the listeners were practicing what I was preaching!

One afternoon I was going through the mail in my office when I came across the newsletter of our community's homeless shelter. Cecil, a longtime servant within the church, had been named "volunteer of the year." This was news to me. Although I frequently saw him around the church, he was not one to draw attention to himself.

Cecil was interviewed in the newsletter about his volunteer activity and was asked about his motivation for such exemplary service. He said, "I have a brother who is a schizophrenic and lives in the Pacific Northwest. He also has paranoid delusions and often feels that people are following him. So he travels from one homeless shelter to another in that part of the country, and sometimes he writes me letters from wherever he is at the time. When I serve the homeless here, I imagine that one of them is my brother."

Of course, one of them is his brother! Matthew 25 is a reminder that Jesus meets us in the complicated places where people really live: "I was hungry and you gave me food, I was thirsty and you gave me something to drink, I was a stranger and you welcomed me, I was naked and you gave me clothing, I was sick and you took care of me, I was in prison and you visited me" (Matt. 25:35-36 NRSV).

In its spiritual life, a congregation is sometimes called to say yes or no to the culture. The reading, hearing, and proclaiming of scriptures shapes a congregation over time. Immersion in the Bible, through experiences such as Disciple, helps ordinary people reflect on the Christian practices that are already happening in the world.

When this is in place, we are able to withstand the latest fads that are marketed in our culture, such as *The Late Great Planet Earth, Left Behind*, and *The Prayer of Jabez*. Each of these surely contains a grain of truth: the Bible calls us to be ready, to watch, to pray for God's blessing and protection. Yet there is a great deal more to the practice of the faith, and this is the birthright of the mainline churches at their best.

In congregations like Mount Tabor and Providence, new persons are often received into membership from a variety of church backgrounds. A couple may be drawn to the youth ministry or the music, or they may be fleeing a bad experience in another parish. They may have little or no appreciation for a denominational tradition. In addition, many lifelong United Methodists have almost no grounding in their own heritage. They may be unaware of John Wesley's commitment to the poor or of the great hymns of his brother Charles.

It was important that we reflect on *The Prayer of Jabez* in light of an important prayer in our own tradition, the covenant prayer. The covenant prayer more accurately articulated an understanding of who we were, the God with whom we were in relationship, and how we might practice our faith in the world. And while an academic might see a book like *The Prayer of Jabez* as trivial or unworthy of attention, a parish minister cannot have a similar perspective, because it is present in the culture of the community and, at times, the congregation.

Paradoxically, God did expand the territory of a group of disciples who were shaped by a prayer that asked for nothing other than to be of service to God's will and purpose. As a congregation, Mount Tabor listened to the words of another prayer that has been practiced for 250 years, a prayer that has been transformative to millions of believers across the generations, many of whom know the fulfillment of the covenant prayer's concluding petition:

> I am no longer my own, but thine.
> Put me to what thou wilt, rank me with whom thou wilt.
> Put me to doing, put me to suffering.
> Let me be employed for thee or laid aside for thee,
> Exalted for thee or brought low for thee.
> Let me be full, let me be empty.
> Let me have all things, let me have nothing.
> I freely and heartily yield all things to thy pleasure and disposal.
> And now, O glorious and blessed God, Father, Son and Holy Spirit,
> Thou art mine and I am thine. So be it.
> And the covenant which I have made on earth,
> Let it be ratified in heaven. Amen.[6]

Providence and The Passion of the Christ

I arrived at Providence Church in the summer of 2003. Providence is a large congregation distinguished by excellent worship, a formal liturgy, a strong tradition of choral music, significant outreach to the community (housing a homeless shelter within its facilities) and world (a twenty-five year partnership with a Haitian community and church), and comprehensive age-level ministries. Providence is located near the heart of the center of Charlotte, North Carolina, which is a fascinating religious culture within itself: Jim and Tammy Bakker became famous in Charlotte, but the progressive Baptist preacher Carlyle Marney spent a number of years in the community as well. I am told by friends that more Presbyterians live in Charlotte than in any other city in the United States, and church attendance in general is high. Within a three-mile radius of Providence there are eighteen congregations with active memberships above one thousand.

This context is a ripe one for religious trends, and the prepublicity and release of the Mel Gibson film *The Passion of the Christ* created something of a stir in our congregation and community. Some of the congregations in our area were renting movie theaters, purchasing blocks of tickets, and attending in large groups. Other congregations were encouraging their members to invite unchurched friends to view the movie with them. A number of pastors in our region were developing series of sermons around the themes of *The Passion of the Christ*.

I had formed an impression of the movie, prior to its release, through various news reports and questions raised by these reports: Was it anti-Semitic? Did Pope John Paul II give the film his endorsement? Was it biblically accurate? Was it unnecessarily violent? I quickly realized that I would need to see the film and formulate some kind of response to it. This I did. I also became aware, along the way, that the film would in some way test the practices that were in place in our congregation.

I saw *The Passion of the Christ* at the beginning of Lent 2004. Our congregation planned a teaching session on the following Wednesday evening. Over two hundred were present. We spent some time reflecting on key issues related to the film: Christians could choose to agree or disagree on such things as whether they liked the film; answers to the question of "Why did Jesus die?"; the writings of Anne Catherine Emmerich and their role in the film; particular inaccuracies related to Scripture (the role of Mary Magdalene, for example); the characterization of Jesus, Mary, and the devil; the questions of excessive violence; and anti-Semitism. We then reflected on the question, "Should I go to this movie?" My own answer was "no." And my further response had something to do with practices. More about that later.

We then broke up into three smaller groups (although they were admittedly too large—such is the reality of our fascination with popular religious trends). In these smaller groups, individuals who had seen the film were asked to make comments. One woman said that she found it to be the most spiritually moving experience of her life; a man confessed that he was numb in response to the violence within five minutes of the movie's beginning.

Having advised people in our congregation to avoid the movie, I am aware that many people saw it: it took in $300 million. I took my notes, circulated them via our church's website, and later appeared on a local television broadcast (along with a Catholic priest more sympathetic than I). I was asked to address a large adult Sunday school class on Palm Sunday on the subject, and I did.

The practice of "saying no" to Mel Gibson's *The Passion of the Christ* (and less than one-third of those present in these gatherings related to this topic had seen it or planned to see it) had to be coupled with "saying yes" to something else—in my mind something more substantive, more biblical, more life-giving. Individuals were encouraged to read the Gospels for themselves, particularly the endings of Mark, Matthew, and Luke, and then John. On one occasion I asked them to make a similar spiritual commitment of three hours to the time it took me to watch the film.

Providence Church is known for its excellence in music, and I also invited members to listen to settings of the Mass (Bach or Beethoven) or the Requiem (Mozart or Rutter). A number of persons chose to do this. Members were asked to form images, in their own minds, of persons in our own community and world who were suffering: the homeless who sleep in our church three nights each week during the winter, the victims of floods in Haiti, where we serve several times each year. These practices, music, and relationships with the poor are deeply embedded in our Methodist tradition.

We also attempted to articulate the importance of our Holy Week schedule, particularly Maundy Thursday and the Good Friday

Tenebrae services. The latter service in particular was often given as a reason by the many who did not want to see *The Passion of the Christ*. One woman noted simply that she did not want to see images from a movie when she was sitting in darkness listening to the last words of Jesus. In those services, which have been a part of the church's experience over many years, we sang hymns from the Methodist tradition, including "O Love Divine, What Hast Thou Done?" by Charles Wesley. This passion hymn, in particular, forms a parallel to the earlier relationship of the prayer of Jabez and the covenant prayer.

Saying Yes and Saying No

Both Mount Tabor and Providence United Methodist Churches are at something of a crossroads. Each has a rich heritage, drawing from two hundred years of a particular theological tradition (Wesleyan) and three thousand years of the biblical tradition. Each exists in something of a spiritual marketplace, in which Christian communities coexist, often with very different visions of the faith. Increasingly, all North American Christian churches find themselves in a larger context that is shaped by media forces that are pervasive and at times overwhelming.

My learning from these two congregations is that they did have a cluster of practices in place and that these practices had been present over a number of years. Some of them have been noted: Disciple Bible Study, liturgical worship, significant outreach. The sense of identity within these congregations allowed them to reflect critically on the culture that was attempting to shape them. As a preacher, I recognize that I too make decisions vis-à-vis the culture: Will I preach a series of sermons related to *The Prayer of Jabez*, or *The Passion of the Christ*? Probably not. Do I stay with the lectionary? Probably. And yet I am convinced that I ignore phenomena like *The Prayer of Jabez* and *The Passion of the Christ* at my own peril. These works do shape the spiritual lives of many, including a number of persons who are members of Mount Tabor and Providence churches. And it is possible that God uses these resources to lead persons toward a deeper faith.

My own calling, as a pastor in a mainline Christian congregation, is to search for an alternative. Over time I have sensed that many persons who are involved in mainline churches, at least the ones I have served, have both a healthy skepticism about current religious trends and a deep desire for a more authentic faith. My search often leads me back to sources that have been life giving for me and for those who have gone before me. Healthy mainline churches have rich and substantive practices in place, and individuals in these two congregations were able to reconnect with them even in the midst of powerful movements in the spiritual marketplace.

We can say no to a Christian product or resource; we sometimes, in fact, feel called in some way to do so. We can also say yes to something more truthful, more profound. We are invited to stay close to the tree that is planted by streams of living water (Psalm 1), for only there will we not be tossed about by the prevailing winds (James 1) of the spiritual marketplace. A congregation rooted in the practices of the faith is able to test the spirits and to discern the way that leads to life.

Notes

1. See Kenneth H. Carter Jr., *A Way of Life in the World* (Nashville: Abingdon, 2004), 91.
2. Reuben Job, *A Wesleyan Spiritual Reader* (Nashville: Abingdon, 1998), 194–95.
3. Bruce Wilkinson, *The Prayer of Jabez: Breaking through to the Blessed Life* (Sisters, OR: Multnomah, 2000).
4. These words are taken from the Covenant Renewal Service in the Wesleyan tradition. They were published in 1753 by John Wesley and can be traced to a Puritan text written almost one hundred years earlier. The first covenant service in the Methodist movement was probably celebrated in 1755, according to *The United Methodist Book of Worship*. The service has been

a popular one on New Year's Eve, New Year's Day, and on the first Sunday of a New Year (Keith Beasley-Topliffe, *Surrendering to God* [Brewster, MA: Paraclete Press, 2001], esp. pp. 1–12).

5. Dorothy C. Bass, ed., *Practicing Our Faith: A Way of Life for Searching People*, Jossey-Bass Practicing Our Faith Series (San Francisco: Jossey-Bass, 1998), 5.

6. *The United Methodist Hymnal* (Nashville: United Methodist Publishing House, 1989), 607.

Navigating Culture

Polycultures and Digital Culture in the Postmodern Age

Steve Jacobsen
Goleta Presbyterian Church
Goleta, California

> *Goleta Presbyterian Church sits behind a shopping center in Goleta, California, Santa Barbara's less glamorous suburban neighbor to the west. Sitting near a large state university, Goleta reflects California's quintessential blend of the rootless information age and bewildering cultural diversity. Drawing on the metaphor of farming, Steve Jacobsen shares how growing a spiritual community in this diverse and technological environment takes practice but can lead to a hardy spiritual yield.*

I've changed my opinion about what a good garden looks like. I used to evaluate a garden in terms of size, the straightness of the rows, and the amount of weeds and volunteer species growing in it. Now I have learned to look for other things in a garden—how sustainable it is, how well it reflects the local ecosystem, and how well it can adapt to change. As my sense of what makes a good garden has changed, so has my sense of what makes a good church.

When I seek metaphors to understand how my congregation has evolved over the last thirteen years, I'm drawn to the descriptions of sustainable agriculture used by the novelist Wendell Berry and the soil scientist Wes Jackson.

In *Jayber Crow*, Wendell Berry chronicles several generations of life in the fictional town of Port William, Kentucky. Among the many memorable characters are an older farmer named Athey Keith and his restless son-in-law, Troy. Athey's farm has been in his family for several generations. When Athey considers what to do with his farm each year, he keeps in mind what it can sustain. This understanding is based on a detailed knowledge of the farm's past, its limitations, and its capacities. Athey has acquired this knowledge slowly, through careful observation and interaction year after year. Athey has a genuine reverence for the land. Eventually his daughter marries Troy, and due to declining health, Athey passes the farm on to him. Troy has a different view of farming. He is driven by a hunger for dramatic change and profit. If he can't "make it big" as a large-scale farmer, life will not be worth living. His impatience and anxiety lead him to borrow all he can and invest in expensive equipment. "And so then the equipment, the power to do things mechanically, became his point of reference. His question was what his equipment could do, not what could the farm stand. The farm, in a way, became his mirror."[1]

What Wendell Berry describes in fiction, the soil scientist Wes Jackson describes in scientific terms. When Jackson explains what is missing from the modern understanding of agriculture, he often talks about the importance of *polycultures*. Polycultures are ecological systems that include many species of plant and animal life within a particular region. They have evolved slowly over a period of time. They have withstood many swings and changes in climate and many kinds of pests and disease. The various life-forms depend on each other, drawing from each other in many intricate ways. *Monocultures*, by contrast, occur when polycultures are cleared away in favor of large tracts of land, all planted with the same crop. Monocultures are designed to fit an industrial model of food production. This homogeneity makes it easier to manage—large machinery can be used to plant and harvest, for example. But a monoculture has some fatal flaws. Its lack of diversity makes it vulnerable to pests and diseases that thrive on a particular crop; not having to travel far from host to host, a weevil has an unlimited and convenient source of food and can reproduce at extraordinary rates. The farmer therefore has to spend large amounts of money on pesticides. A polyculture is complex and subtle; it has a collective wisdom that has evolved over time. A monoculture may seem be simpler to understand and manage, but it has lost its wisdom and subtle integrity.

When I came to my current congregation thirteen years ago, I was full of programs, energy, and vision for what we could do and how we could do it. In my rational, ambitious mind, I could envision "great things" happening. Like Troy, I expected my programs and plans would produce dramatic yields. If what was waiting for me then was an easily managed spiritual "monoculture"—people all alike, with similar backgrounds and opinions, all lined up in straight rows ready for development—my job might have been easy. Fortunately, something else happened, and an easily managed monoculture is not what emerged. Looking back thirteen years later, I realize some of the most significant truths and possibilities were not visible to me at the beginning, but hidden in the "soil" of peoples' souls. Some of the important developments would emerge only as we took time to identify and respond to external challenges coming from the larger society, such as the growing influence of technology. All this came slowly over time and in unanticipated ways. I had to give up being like Troy and learn more how to see things through Athey's eyes. Eventually I learned to appreciate and revere the particular "polyculture of the Spirit" that would prove to be right and sustainable in this particular postmodern California community. This is a story about how we have chosen to be faithful and some things I learned in the process.

The first part of the story describes how we have come to understand diversity as a "polyculture of the Spirit." The second part is an account of how we have come to terms with digital culture.

Honoring the Diversity of Spiritual Journeys: Finding a Polyculture of the Spirit

For centuries congregations were formed around ethnic identities. People shared a native language and customs and a well-defined theology. But all that has changed. In the postmodern age, many people look not for what satisfied their parents or grandparents, but what gives them a personal sense of meaning and belonging. Even though I am a Presbyterian pastor, I did not grow up in the Presbyterian church. When I look out at the congregation on a Sunday morning, my guess is that three-quarters of those present are like me—they came from some other denomination (if they were raised within one at all). If there was a day of ethnic/denominational "monocultures," that day has passed. But the loss in homogeneity leads to a richer variety. Let me introduce you to several of the key leaders in my congregation:

- The first person has been the church secretary since I arrived. A former elementary school teacher and "cradle Presbyterian," she went through a painful divorce a few years after I arrived. Out of that pain emerged a new sense of herself, and the calling for service in the church that she'd had since childhood began to grow stronger. It became clear that she had a gift for words, spiritual insights, and leading worship. She has become a gifted lay preacher.
- The second person grew up in a Catholic family. During the sixties, his spiritual hunger, coupled with a deep dismay over the public "media face" of Christianity at the time, led him to leave his Christian roots to investigate many traditions. He ended up getting a doctorate in crosscultural religious studies. For many years he considered himself a Buddhist. He came to our congregation reluctantly, only because his fiancée wanted to be married in a Presbyterian church. He ended up staying, becoming involved, and emerging as a key leader. A love for Christ he knew as a child has reemerged with new clarity and depth. He has become one of our members who teaches people in our church and in the larger community how to incorporate Buddhist meditation practices into Christian faith.

- The third person grew up in the Methodist church. He was a project manager with a local defense contractor and appreciated being part of this congregation. One day, however, he had a charismatic experience—a profound sense of being filled with light and the love of God. This spiritual experience led him to see his faith not as just one part of his life, but the very foundation of his identity and purpose. He has become a founder of a healing prayer ministry and a dedicated Bible study leader.

- The fourth person grew up in a home without any interest in Christian faith. She first came to a youth retreat fifteen years ago because she wanted to meet boys. Becoming involved in the youth ministry program, she found the youth pastor was often available to listen to her reflect on her life. She eventually shared with him some painful experiences she had as a child. He listened to her and became her advocate. By the time the youth pastor left, she had begun to go her own way and drifted away from the church. But she ended up coming back occasionally to worship, then more often, and then joined as an adult member. She became an elder and cochair of a search committee for a new youth director. When we were not finding the right person, she felt led to become a candidate. We hired her. For the last four years, she has been doing an excellent job in that role. Now, after an extended time of introspection, she is preparing for seminary and eventual ordination.

- The fifth person grew up in a single parent family. She had been taught by her mother to distrust institutions of all kinds. After college she got married in Boston. Her husband had been raised Catholic, and they wanted to have a ceremony that had a spiritual reverence without being too doctrinal. They chose a Quaker-style service. After moving back to California, she and her husband began looking for a church. They wanted something with more content than a Quaker service but less ritual than a Catholic mass. They eventually became members and, last year both were elected to serve as elders.

Out of these five, only one person was raised in the Presbyterian church. Three went through prolonged periods of skepticism and searching. All five have experienced significant change and development in their understanding of what Christian faith means to them. They work together in many different areas. If you were in conversation with this group, you'd find that they have different views of how to interpret Scripture and the significance of other faiths. They have different political views and opinions about key social issues. They have differing musical tastes. In some ways they represent the eclecticism that California is known for. But despite their differences, they have two things in common: they have come to the door of this particular church and stayed, and if you listen to them tell their stories as I have, you would be persuaded that God's Spirit has been leading them and forming them for a very long time. To me, they represent a "polyculture of the Spirit"—different ways of being Christian, each with an inherent integrity and vitality. When we create programs, study groups, and worship services, we intentionally seek to reflect this diversity we have in our midst.

Music is often a clear indication of a congregation's culture, and this polyculture is expressed in the musical style of our worship services. A decade ago, we relied almost entirely on the Presbyterian hymnbook with an occasional "Kumbaya." Recognizing the growth in popularity of praise music, several years ago we created an alternative service with praise music. What works well for some congregations did not work for us. We abandoned it and went back to search for some kind of blend. Over a period of several years, we tried different combinations. As we experimented, some people left because we were staying too traditional, and some left because we were not staying traditional enough. We had some hurt feelings as one or another musical group felt threatened. But over time we achieved equilibrium and a sense of freedom.

Now, in any particular service, we might use a Bach hymn, a Taizé prayer chant, a gospel hymn, a praise song, and a jazz arrangement for the offertory. The next week the music may be mostly traditional, and the next week mostly praise. But it's not a random or careless process. What we do is based on the theme of the service on a particular day and what musical gifts and resources are available to us. The variety can be disorienting to someone seeking a musical monoculture, but it is part of who we have become. And who we have become is not just the result of a series of compromises, nor it is just a way of being "nice." Instead, it's an intentional way to practice living and worshiping with a group of people with diverse backgrounds. I believe this is not about being polite, but about being faithful. When it works and hangs together, it is an aural expression of the different ways God can be sought, praised, and celebrated. It works for us.

What is true in worship styles is true of the kind of educational opportunities we offer. We have had groups work through material from Willow Creek and Rick Warren as well as books by Marcus Borg. We have healing prayer training led by a local charismatic pastor as well as occasional classes in yoga and meditation techniques. We have speakers describing the power and practice of Christian forgiveness one month and speakers describing the character of different faith traditions during another. We are planning half-day "Teach Me to Pray" events in which participants are introduced to Scripture verse memorization, *lectio divina*, meditation techniques, and Celtic practices. In all this we practice listening to and learning from different voices with the voice of Christ as our constant point of reference.

We find ways to work with these differences in the areas of public affairs and politics. We have a strong, progressive international peace program, the original leadership of which included two friends and golfing partners, one an active Republican and the other an active Democrat. We have invited local politicians to speak at educational events, focusing not on partisan issues but on their views of the future. And in a part of the country that has few visible links to the past—no cemeteries, battlefields, or war memorials—we honor veterans on public holidays as a way to link us to the past while seeking peace and justice in the future.

A good "polyculture farmer" nurtures not only what he or she has decided to plant, but also what new species, growth, and possibilities emerge spontaneously from the land itself. In our congregation, we have become better at recognizing talents, possibilities, and insights that arise apart from our formal planning. For instance, after interviewing several stained-glass artists, the sanctuary design committee realized that nothing being shown to them seemed right. Eventually one of the members of the group, an accomplished water colorist, volunteered to create a design for the first of eight windows. What she came up with was perfect—fresh, fluid, and beautiful. She has gone on to do all the designs.

In another meeting one night, we were discussing how to get the best price on an adjacent piece of land we had decided to sell. One person wondered aloud if we could find a use for the land that would not necessarily get the most money, but would instead be consistent with our mission. We ended up contacting several local nonprofits, which led to selling the land at half the appraised value to the Cerebral Palsy Foundation. They built thirteen units of low-income housing on that land. Several of the residents began attending our church and joining, teaching us in the process important lessons about hospitality. In other words, being attentive to what emerges spontaneously has become as important as paying attention to our more intentionally designed plans and programs. This more improvisational style of ministry seems consistent not only with California culture but with Jesus' ministry—while he had plans and intentions for each day, he was always able to respond to unforeseen events (like someone touching his garment), drawing out of such moments new possibilities and lessons.

To reinforce and nurture this way of being a church, I use some simple educational concepts. One is the circle of the six dimensions of spiritual life developed by Richard Foster and James Bryan Smith in the Renovaré series.[2] Foster and Smith identified major themes in Jesus' life and Christian traditions—contemplative, holiness, charismatic (meant here to include a broad range of Spirit-seeking practices, including the Quaker), social justice, evangelical, and incarnational. Their thesis is that each of us is drawn to one of these traditions and its practices, but all of them have legitimacy and importance. As individuals, we can broaden our spiritual life by understanding and experimenting with themes that are not our "home base," learning at least an understanding and appreciation of each one. As a community, we can recognize that not everyone will be at the same place on the circle as we are, but the perspective and insight of others contributes to a more holistic vision. I have used this concept and others like it (such as the work on "spiritual type" of Corrine Ware[3]) in leadership training, new member classes, small groups, and worship.

The development of our "polyculture character" has given us a particular identity that is evident to visitors. Any visitor will soon sense our approach and convictions. "Nomads" who come seeking this kind of diversity end up staying. Deciding to stay means they are exchanging their nomad identities (wanderers without a home) for pilgrim identities (people on a journey who believe they have a home). That "home" is a reverence for God found in the practice of reverence for one another, as exemplified in Jesus' ministry.

Finding a way to develop a sustainable spiritual polyculture has allowed us to find vitality in the cultural environment of our particular community. This, in itself, is worthwhile. But I believe there is another important benefit. In a society and world that thrives on divisiveness, caricatures, and cynicism, intentionally living in a "polyculture of the Spirit" trains us to look for God's Spirit at work in each person. Instead of seeing how we can reshape others in our own image, we take time to see how Christ is already present and growing in them.

The Promise and Perils of a Digital Culture

A polycultural farm draws vitality and strength not only from its inner diversity, but also from its ability to sense and respond to changes in the surrounding environment. While we have been finding a way to thrive with our differences, we have also been reflecting on the rising influence of digital culture. Since the advent of personal computers, the Internet, and cell phones in the 1990s, technology has been transforming American life. Some of the changes are conspicuous and some are subtle. Some changes appear as blessings; others seem more like curses. We have been wondering together how people of faith can navigate through these strong currents of change to claim the blessings while avoiding the curses. What practices can help us find our way?

Our search began in the fall of 1999 when I attended a local lecture by Thomas Friedman, international correspondent of the *New York Times*. In the presentation, Friedman described the ways in which technology was radically changing modern life. In the question and answer period following, someone asked him, "Where is God in all this?" Although Friedman had not mentioned God or religion in his lecture, he replied that the two most common questions asked of him on his book tour were "Where is God in all this?" and "What are you doing for your children?" He then went on at length describing his new recognition of the importance of religion in general as a source of values and perspective. He said this has led him to a new commitment to teaching his own children the "three Rs" of reading, arithmetic, and religion (or, we might now say, reading, algorithms, and religion). The issues he raised became the focus of a sabbatical study leave I had the next year, as well as the theme of two grant-funded studies I conducted over the next three years. Within the congregations, we had four small groups spend a year exploring how the new technology was affecting family life, work life, and spiritual practices. I went through a three-month preaching series, reflecting on how we can view technology from the perspective of our faith. This research and exploration has influenced our congregational life in many ways.

- I often include references to our overdependence on technology in our liturgy, in both the call to worship and confession of sin. Technology works many wonders for us, particularly in the areas of medicine and communication. But we can become overdependent on it and saturated with it. It can lead us to spend less and less time communicating face-to-face, enjoying nature, doing activities that remind us of our finitude, and engaging in timeless practices (such as Sabbath keeping) that open us up to God.

• In worship we now regularly include periods for silent prayer and meditation in our services, creating a "sanctuary from distraction." I put in the bulletin four or five different suggestions for using the ten minutes of silence—reflect on the sermon, engage in intercessory prayer, use imagination to re-enter the day's story, or simply sit with eyes open and practice being still. These spiritual activities are not new, but creating time to practice them is increasingly rare, and teaching people the basics of how to do them is increasingly important. By practicing together the art of seeking God apart from devices, we build an inner wisdom and spiritual centering that enables us to reenter our device-saturated society with a better perspective.

• Three years ago we moved into a new sanctuary. As we worked with the architects to design the interior, we were faced with the common questions facing many churches today: given the increasing use of computer projection as a worship tool, do we want to create a space like a theater, with a screen in the center and easily darkened? Or do we want to emphasize natural light with large windows? We opted for the second choice but did decide to have a retractable screen installed off center and a digital projector placed behind a rear wall. When we project images, they are not as brilliant as if the room were dark, but we have retained a sense that the sanctuary is an evocative place of worship apart from any devices.

• With this new environment, we have nevertheless been experimenting with how to use new technology in a way that serves our worship purposes. We briefly tried using PowerPoint templates for sermons, employing the standard "bullet point" programs, but decided that, most of the time, it was not for us. ("It makes me feel like I'm back at work," said one engineer.) Another person said that looking up continuously at the screen interrupted her eye contact with the preacher, breaking the "energy flow" and making the worship experience less personal.

- At the same time, I have been using the projection system to display traditional and contemporary artwork and photography as part of the sermon. In a culture where images are used primarily to market products and keep our minds busy, learning to look steadily and carefully at a great work of visual imagination can be a kind of contemplative practice. In the not too distant past, finding good artwork and presenting it involved taking slide photographs, having them developed, and then projecting them, a labor-intensive activity. The Internet makes countless images available and pliable, and projection is easy. Seeing a NASA photograph of the Sea of Galilee from space not only helps people see the geography of the Gospels, but links science with faith. Looking carefully at a Giotto, Rembrandt, Van Gogh, or Chagall, as well as an African folk painting, Indonesian batik, or the artwork of a child in the congregation, is an experience that is neither manipulative nor shallow, but rather evocative, revelatory, and meaningful, and can be a delightful and inspirational experience. Being calm and looking carefully can reveal truths we will miss if we are in a hurry—an important spiritual skill we can use in many facets of our lives. Seeing a biblical story through the eyes and imagination of different artists from different cultures and a different era can help us understand that any given story can have multiple meanings—an important lesson in itself.

- So far we have resisted the frequent use of videos and movies. The younger a person is today, the more his or her primary way of receiving information is through video and fast-paced digital imagery. Many churches use it extensively because it helps people have a seamless transition from the world of television and movies to the experience of worship. For me the concern has been what I can best describe by thinking about neural stimulation. When we are watching a video, we receive a quick succession of images that have been carefully chosen and edited for maximum effect. Our brain finds it very difficult not to be engaged, and our own ability to judge the narrative the editor has used is compromised. While a video or movie can be memorable and persuasive, it keeps us dependent on external stimulation rather than internal discernment. If I am trying to nurture my own capacity to form meaning and make judgments, I am not being helped.

- We do use the screen as needed to project lyrics to music we are singing, but we avoid any clever effects. While some don't like lyrics projected, some older members find the screen easier to read, and some disabled members find that it frees them from having to hold a hymnal.

- As new people come into membership, I include some of our approach to technology in the early sessions of new member classes. I ask people to choose from a list of simple practices and experiment for a week with living more intentionally in the digital culture, turning some things off to make room for other activities. Once we begin to see how much our behavior, lifestyles, and stress levels are influenced by technology and our hyperactive culture, and begin to experience some ability to make choices about it, we are readier to see worship, service, and fellowship activities as spiritual practices that require intentional focus.

Like an invisible force field, technology is reshaping our personal, family, and communal lives. In our congregation we have tried to reflect carefully about technology's promises and perils, using as our point of reference not what is quick and easy but what is consistent with the values of the kingdom of God. This, in itself, is an important spiritual practice.

Conclusion

Creating a polyculture of the Spirit and responding thoughtfully to the growing influence of technology have kept us busy as, week to week, we find what works and what doesn't. In this sense, these things have become "practices" that we engage in, which over time have formed our congregational identity and ministry. Both have become part of who we are, but neither is an end in itself.

Looking back, I realize that seeking our own way of "being church" has helped me draw closer to God. As I listen to different people tell their spiritual stories, I am always moved by God's attentiveness to the details of peoples' lives and the different directions God can lead people. And working through our concerns about technology draws me more deeply into Scripture and tradition as we look for clues of what faithful living looks like in the digital age. In other words, being on this journey continues to deepen my reverence for God's presence, power, and wisdom. And that reminds me of good farming. When Troy looked at the land, he saw his own ambitions; when Athey looked at the same land, he found a source of endless wonder.

Notes

1. Wendell Berry, *Jayber Crow* (New York: Counterpoint Press, 2000), 338.
2. These streams are described on the Renovaré Web site, www.renovare.org, and in books in the Renovaré series from HarperSanFrancisco, such as James Bryan Smith and Richard J. Foster, *A Spiritual Formation Workbook: Small Group Resources for Nurturing Christian Growth*, rev. ed. (San Francisco: HarperSanFrancisco, 1999).
3. Corinne Ware, *Discover Your Spiritual Type: A Guide to Individual and Congregational Growth* (Herndon, VA: Alban, 1995).

ENGAGING CREATIVITY

Journey to the Unfamiliar

Todd M. Donatelli
The Cathedral of All Souls
Asheville, North Carolina

The Episcopal Cathedral of All Souls in Asheville, North Carolina, enjoys a unique history among American churches. Completed in 1896, this architectural gem was constructed as the focus of the artisan village adjoining George Vanderbilt's impressive Biltmore Estate. From its very conception, All Souls has been a place where arts and crafts have been celebrated. But it might be easy to take this heritage for granted. In this essay, Todd Donatelli tells how intentionally embracing the arts as a spiritual practice has transformed All Souls and helped its members look at the world in new ways.

The arts and human creativity have never been more important. They are not simply skills; their concern is the intellectual and spiritual maturity of human life. We hope that through offerings of concerts, exhibits, dramatic productions, literary offerings, and educational lectures the experiencing, sharing, and appreciation of the arts will not be the luxury of a few, but the best hope of humanity to experience joy on this planet. The mission of the cathedral Arts Commission is to present arts offerings within the cathedral setting not exclusively for ritualistic activity in worship and liturgy, but as worship itself.

—The Arts Commission of the Cathedral of All Souls

> Art is an adventure into an unknown world that can be explored
> only by those willing to take risks.
>
> —Mark Rothko

When our oldest daughter was two years old, we took her to the local
Greek Festival. After dancing and eating wonderful food, we walked
into the sanctuary. As we entered the space, this bubbling, giggling
child riding my back, still moving to the rhythms of Greek music,
suddenly froze, her eyes transfixed on the ceiling. "Look!" was all she
could say, pointing to the magnificent mosaic of the face of Christ
that covered the entirety of the massive ceiling. She would not move
and did not want us to move. After a long period of silence, she
asked, "Who is that?" "Jesus" we replied. I recall wondering if this
massive image would spook her in some way, yet her body and face
said something else. She did not want to leave, but kept on looking at
the image as if in some way conversing with the presence she felt.

What is it about art and the arts that can grab our souls, connect
us to the transcendent, and invite us to a place of secure unknowing?
In our baptismal liturgy, we ask God to give those baptized "the gift
of joy and wonder in all your works."[1] How is it that the arts are so
able to take us to places of wonder?

In this chapter I will tell of the life-transforming power of the
arts at the Cathedral of All Souls. I will do so often through the words
of parishioners who have been invited to reflect on what it is about
the arts that defines, informs, and inspires this community and them.

In this telling I am also conscious of what brought me to this
cathedral eight years ago: the congregation's earthiness, their readi-
ness to risk, explore, and imagine, and their willingness to allow the
edges of their common life to be a bit rough, knowing that divine
connection with human yearning is not always smooth and predictable. The Cathedral of All Souls is a community that is not as concerned about whether something goes right or what others will think
as much as whether we have stretched ourselves to consider something we, to this point, may not have seen or known. It is a community that trusts in the presence of the Spirit and trusts that God is

one who creates. It is a community that believes that for those created in the image of God, a sign of their fruitfulness, a sign of their engagement with the Spirit, will be creativity incarnate.

In the Beginning

"Our cathedral is embracing in its architecture . . . a beautifully built building of the finest materials. The result over a century later is a setting with a rich patina that only adds depth to the spiritual embrace of this community."—Millie Elmore

When George Vanderbilt was building a "country estate" in the mountains of Asheville, North Carolina, he asked his architect, Richard Morris Hunt, to design a church for the village adjacent to the home. Using themes from Romanesque, Gothic, and Norman architecture, he created a worship space that is at once linear and circular. Its lines are simple yet profound. The space draws people in and leaves no one feeling that he or she is "in the back." Its lines are steep and intimate. The materials—brick, granite, oak, and brass—are solid and delicately tooled. The windows are vibrant, with other village structures designed not to impede the sunlight passing through. The space is the first work of art one encounters upon entering the cathedral.

Perhaps inspired by this foundation or drawn to it, members of All Souls have been creating ever since. The tallest point of the roofline is capped by an iron cross, again incorporating linear and circular lines, created by Marianne Zabriskie, wife of the cathedral's first dean, Neil Zabriskie. The banners, paschal candle stand, votive candle stand, tract rack, kneelers, vessels for communion, and vestments are among the elements the church commissioned local artists, both members and nonmembers, to create. Offerings of drama, concerts, literary readings with authors, art exhibitions, films, and literary journals proclaim, "This is a place for the creative."

The cathedral's tradition of arts engagement, support, and offerings begins with Vanderbilt and continues with other significant developments, such as the hiring of Marilyn Kaiser as organist and choirmaster in the 1960s. She was an associate to Alec Wyton at St. John the Divine, and her position drew Mr. Wyton himself to All Souls on many occasions. This congregation has also hosted benefit concerts for the Asheville Symphony Chorus and other local arts groups. All Souls may be the only church in town to purchase advertising in the city's theater and opera programs. The cathedral's tradition of involvement in the arts attracts members who are participants in the city's dramatic, instrumental, choral, and visual arts venues as well as local college arts professors. All Souls has continuously opened itself throughout its history to the possibilities and generation of imagination that come through the arts.

Transformation and Imagination

"Walking into a space that is quiet and beautiful, catching your favorite window at the right time of day, hearing an anthem by Tallis or Mozart or a poem by one of our own, seeing a banner wrought by skillful and loving hands and silver and ceramic communion vessels crafted by local artisans—these are the things that make a difference in the life of the cathedral, and that difference is most likely incalculable."—David Jordan

"Beautiful, professionally executed music transforms the cathedral into an icon; the ethereal sounds becoming the eyes of Christ that draw us into the great mystery of the Divine."—Ted Ahl

When security or a "return to fundamentals" becomes a compelling voice of the community, how do we invite people to venture into a "new world"? How can we believe there is a new world and that it is a place of life?

Perhaps we are saved from thinking too highly of our period in history, or despairing of it, by remembering the Renaissance, arguably one of the greatest time periods of human creativity and imagination. The historical context? Florence, Italy, a locus of so much of the creativity of that time, was beset by regular plagues, constant wars accompanied by oppressive taxation to support the wars, and blockades that kept goods and materials from flowing to places that could support their economy. Amid this backdrop came a generation of imagination that inspires the human soul to this day.

While we are certainly not the first generation of human beings to be tempted by the siren songs of "security" and the bolstering of "fundamentals," we certainly live in an age when exploration in theology and human understanding creates much anxiety. This is not simply an issue for "those" people—whoever "those" may be—but for us who, like Adam and Eve, try to hide in our fear and become disconnected from ourselves and that which surrounds us.

An old mentor used to ask regularly, "What allows you to outflank your natural defenses?" By this he was asking, in what contexts do you feel safe enough to listen when your natural defenses might say otherwise? The arts have offered attendees of All Souls a safe context in which to try things on and imagine what they invite, with the knowledge that the excursion can be brief. The knowing of this beforehand, that we are safe to enter and exit, seems to allow us to remain with the exploration longer than we might naturally.

Transformation and Liturgy

"I am continually amazed at the ability of hymn texts and anthem texts to move me to tears, slipping around every defense I possess and rocketing right to my heart."—Ted Ahl

"Every Sunday that we attend services at All Souls is an artistic as well as a spiritual event."—Millie Elmore

How do the arts help us to "hear things slant" in liturgy? We may never allow ourselves to dance on a stage, yet we can venture in with the ones offering their movement in ways that they become a place to take our yearnings, our fears, our desire to reach out, and our temptation to look away. In their movement, we can sample and explore our own.

A couple of years ago, David Hopes, professor of literature at University of North Carolina–Asheville, a member of All Souls and often the director of our Palm Sunday Passion, suggested we invite a local dance professional to interpret the story of Christ's passion. The idea was for the dancer to be moving and interpreting while someone read the text. Even those who did not care much for dance in liturgy were profoundly moved by one particularly poignant moment. When during the narration we heard, "One of you will betray me," the reader paused, and the dancer slowly turned to the congregation and, with index finger eloquently extended in a direct point, began a slow sweep of all gathered, inviting us to contemplate how we too participate in the betrayal of Jesus. It is easy to become "dreamingly innocent" when we listen to the Passion narrative, yet no one could honestly hide from the accusing point of this person. Her bodily posture brought the story into our flesh in a manner that its simple reading might not.

Often when we sing "All Creatures of Our God and King," we stop the music on verse 6 and rather than sing the line, hear it read. "And even you, most gentle death, waiting to hush our final breath, O praise him, Alleluia! You lead back home the child of God, for Christ our Lord that way has trod: O praise him, Alleluia!" The ceasing of music and reading of the line offers a change, a disruption, synchronistic with the disruption of death. In this act we are not invited simply to continue singing, but to enact in our bodies what we are proclaiming with our lips. Again we are invited to be present to the Word as it seeks to speak afresh in ancient texts.

The arts can also speak and connect us to the Divine when we are weary or simply have no words to offer. Preparing for the liturgy on the evening of 9/11, we found ourselves looking to texts, music, and aesthetic appearance to speak to that which we were still trying to comprehend, let alone try and name. When we prepared a service for its first anniversary, we again looked to texts, anthems, and visual images that straddled the fine line of remembrance and despair, hope and triumphalism. It was contemplation of the images, texts, music, and physical movement, the aesthetic of the liturgy, that saved us from an idolatrous hubris and called us to listening, reflection, and the offering of ourselves.

"In the recitals and concerts offered at All Souls and particularly in our liturgy, we experience the carefully considered and articulated poetic and musical expressions of saints and sinners, great and obscure, who have gone before us and have left us a tangible expression of their faith and their service employed in the act of worship. I find particular strength and power in texts that challenge and inspire composers as powerfully today as decades and centuries before us. The stability of these expressions provides a foundation for my beliefs and informs my worship."—Ted Ahl

Intentionality with the artistic compels us to consider regularly how we might offer something afresh. It delivers us from the stifling security of not wishing to risk anew. How might we offer this hymn, this text, this sermon? How might the space appear different? What movement of the congregation, of individual persons, could introduce a new dimension to this proclamation? Artistic expression invites us to consider how all of our body and soul might interact with the Word being proclaimed in that moment. Carefully considered expressions invite new telling of the "old, old story."

A Trip to Florence

In the summer of 2003, my family and I had the opportunity to spend a month in Italy during a sabbatical. Thanks to St. James Episcopal Church in Florence and its rector, Peter Casparian, we were able to spend the bulk of that time in Florence. Shortly before leaving Asheville, I was visiting with Ridgeway and Mary Lynch, two longtime members of All Souls. Ridgeway, an engineer by vocation, handed me a book entitled "Brunelleschi's Dome." It tells the story about construction of the dome on the Cathedral of Santa Maria del Fiore in Florence. Ridgeway suggested I might find the story fascinating. He could not have realized how that book and the *duomo* would become one of the primary icons for that sabbatical.

When construction of the cathedral began in the fourteenth century, its design called for a dome the size of which had not successfully

been built since the completion of the Pantheon. Because part of the
nave of the cathedral was being used at the time of the dome com-
missioning, those offering the commission made it clear that no internal support could be used in construction. What does it take to lay
a foundation and begin construction of a building to support something the details and needs of which you do not yet know? That question became one of the primary ponderings of my sabbatical. How
does a community step into a calling and discern and begin laying a
"foundation" for it when the ultimate details of that calling cannot
yet be known? What does it take to live like this?

To create the chosen design, Filippo Brunelleschi looked to the
past, to foundations, to find the insight for his yet to be imagined
vision. He traveled to Rome and received permission (some of it
perhaps unofficial) to excavate foundations of the great arches and
domes. From this reintegration of the past, he dreamed of a dome
which to this day is a primary symbol of the imagination and bril-
liance of the Renaissance period.

I see in this story a correlation between engaging creative works
from the past and imagining a "new thing" in the present.
Brunelleschi, an artist as well as an engineer, incarnated this connection. He pursued a reconsideration, a reengagement of the past that
could inspire a new imagining of the present. Engaging the artistic
imagination of those who had gone before stimulated his own ability
to wonder and dream.

The arts are able to connect us also to foundations that inspire
new imagination. We need not "free ourselves from the past" to imagine the "new," as if the past is somehow confining. It is as if there is
some inherent imagination in these prior works that evoke our current imagination. Be it a Bach composition, a Gregorian chant, a
monk's frescoes, Christian services of light, the poetry of Jewish scripture, or icons commissioned by the church in medieval times, we
have a wealth of artistic expression that feeds our connection to God's
imagination. Instead of "cleansing" ourselves of works from the past,
as did so many during the Reformation, works of the past can be that

from which we find more deepened encounters with God today. Their imagination can provoke ours.

"The arts see transcendent beauty and reveal it to this world. In their vision of eternal beauty they can impart eternity to the things of time. . . . The arts aspire to be not merely a 'comfort,' but also a real and transforming power: in the words of Dostoevsky: 'beauty will redeem the world.'"[2]

What does it take to imagine that which we cannot see? What does it take to step into a vision, the details of which we cannot yet know? I believe the arts provoke sojourning wonder.

Arts and the Attraction of Souls

"I think our focus on the arts draws interesting people to this church."—Cheryl Smith

"I came to All Souls to sing in the choir. Attention to beauty and the arts both attracts new members to the church and holds current members."—David Fortney

"Art and architecture you might say helped to lead us to All Souls and opened the doors to a deeper spiritual life."—Millie Elmore

"I know that there are people who have by chance attended All Souls and recognized that our worship experience gives them something that they do not find commonly elsewhere."—Ted Ahl

As people created in the image of God, we connect to God in the creative. Theodore of Studios, speaking in the eighth century about the painting of icons, said, "Man himself is created after the image of God; therefore there is something divine in the art of making images."[3] This might be said of all creative works. All Souls has no trouble attracting local artists to participate in specific offerings and has been the vehicle of affiliation for many.

Another aspect of the cathedral's life that both defines who we are to the local community and attracts them to our steps is the annual village arts and crafts fair, which began in the early 1970s. On the first weekend of August, more than one hundred artists and crafters, local and regional, bring their paintings, ceramic vessels, woven clothing and artwork, wood and metal sculptures, jewelry, and other pieces of art to the lawn of the cathedral. Situated under the century-old trees, they offer their works to thousands of persons who walk the grounds. The fair is overseen by Jon Cram, who owns numerous art galleries as well as the Fine Arts Theatre in Asheville. The fair is one of the premier events of artistic talent in Asheville. In addition to upholding the importance of art in our community, we have also built relationships with many of the artists over the years who find themselves appreciative of connecting to this faith community. They speak of the ways in which this fair declares the sacredness of their work.

On Christmas Eve of 1997, the Church of the Advocate was born in a homeless shelter in Asheville. It is a community of persons "who reside in shelters, people who are housed and people without any sort of resting place of their own."[4] Gathered with the help of a priest and deacon affiliated with All Souls, this group has transformed those who participate in its worship and other gatherings. It has transformed our diocese, causing us to review and rewrite our canons to make room for "worshiping communities," communities that have a seat and vote at diocesan conventions though they do not fit the canonical definition of a parish. In addition to showing and selling artwork created by members of the Advocate at All Souls art shows, members of the Advocate have produced a CD of their own music. Having secured a grant for its production, they split the proceeds between the artists and a local shelter. These same artists often offer their music as anthems and preludes for our worship, an engagement that has converted us and them from strangers to friends. I think All Souls' history of creative imagination opens possibilities such as the Church of the Advocate.

The cathedral Arts Commission has been responsible for hosting book signings and readings, film series, and art shows of parish members as well as members of the Church of the Advocate. In these last two art shows, they have sought and called forth the artistic talents of many who may never have thought to display their work. I see this also as transformative, persons finding affirmation of their work and affirmation of the souls from which these works have sprung. The art shows serve to connect people with God, themselves, and the community.

In the late 1990s, when we commissioned a new paschal candle stand, we wished to uphold a long tradition of supporting artists in the region and engaging an artist with a sense of our context. A blacksmith named Daniel Miller was invited to create the piece. His work incorporates lines of yearning as well as signs of wounds and connection, drawing on the theme of Lent into Easter. Where holes were created for pieces to connect, Daniel chose to hammer rather than drill them, for as he says, "My sense is that in the realm of God, even in wounds, nothing is lost." Like any fine artist, Daniel took time to discuss with us what we wished in the work, did his own research into the symbolism of the Easter vigil and baptismal and burial rites, and brought us ideas of his own that incorporated the symbolic traditions of Christian initiation and birth as well as universal religious ideas.

We found ourselves transformed by Daniel's creation. We invited the congregation to a forum where Daniel spoke about the stand and what it meant to him both in terms of the design and the process of creation. This experience was similar to that which we found in other commissions, such as vestments, eucharistic vessels, a wrought iron votive candle stand, and a tract rack carved by a local artisan. These works connect us to the artists, to our context, and to the transcendent.

In the book *Crossroads: Art and Religion in American Life*, Meredith Monk laments the loss of arts in education and the sense that they are seen as less essential than other areas in our children's development.[5] Hopefully the prominence of offerings such as the arts fair and promotions of the arts and artists in our region proclaim their essentiality for us as people who are in the process of growing into connected, transformed individuals and communities.

The Arts and Our Spiritual Practices

"Because I have two school-age children, our life is at a very busy point. As I sat peacefully in the evensong service, listening to the music with the late afternoon sunshine illuminating the stained-glass windows, I realized I need to make time for this more often."
—Cheryl Smith

"When I offer special music at the Cathedral of All Souls, I consider the opportunity a gift from the congregation. That my fellow parishioners will honor me by allowing me to become part of their worship experience as we praise God and pray together is an awesome responsibility and a humbling opportunity."—Susan Weatherford

"I think art is a refined form of prayer."—David Hopes

Be it an art show on a summer weekend, an evensong on a Sunday afternoon, or the choral recital of a local high school or college group that chooses to use our space, we find in the arts the invitation to stop and reflect. They call us to be present to life in a way that cannot be rushed. We sense their experience and symbols will not be quickly catalogued, categorized, or "day-timed." They demand that we be still and see beyond that which is quickly perceived.

The offering of artistic expression in our community allows for the mutuality of stewardship. It allows us once again to save stewardship from being defined as a fall budget event. When we offer our talents and find them received and part of the community's transformation, we connect with that in us which God has created and in which God delights.

We experience the invitation to offer more of ourselves when any part of the self has been recognized and received. This is certainly true of All Souls where creative offering is not limited to arts, but encompasses outreach, education, pastoral care, and care for our own environs.

As our own gifts and offerings are welcomed, we find the ability to welcome both the unfamiliar and strangers. I think this accounts for All Souls being a place of hospitality and refuge for so many "strangers" in our community. Persons who live on the streets, persons without economic status, persons of same gender orientation, and persons experiencing mental health needs are among those with whom All Souls has identified throughout its history. I think our willingness to explore and willingness to look beyond the known has allowed us to identify with people and issues before they became "popular." The arts discipline us to look beyond the obvious and see beauty and worth in both the familiar and unfamiliar.

> "I have found that it takes time for me to become comfortable with types of music I had not been exposed to before. While I knew it was well done, it took me some time to learn to experience the music as worship. At our latest Easter service, I was at times almost overcome by the power and the emotion communicated through the music. It did not strike me that the choir was doing anything differently from previous years; they were always as excellent, but I was more ready to hear them."—J. Clarkson

Final Thoughts

We have been beckoned and transformed by God through our engagement with the arts. We have learned to acknowledge their primal language. The arts take us to places of the sacred connection with the stranger, be that stranger God, another person, or ourselves.

We at All Souls are fortunate to live in an area of the country where each day is another experience of the ever-revealing Word in creation. Each day reveals a painted canvas as the sun retreats behind the mountains of western North Carolina. We are surrounded by streams and falls that have been running for millennia and will continue to do so long after we are gone. It is no surprise that this is an area of great artistic talent and expressed yearning. It is no surprise that this is a place that provokes wonder, for it is a place of connection to the earth, the past, the present, and our future. It is a place whose very rocks cry out, "Life." It seems our task is to stand before creation and listen.

Notes

1. *The Book of Common Prayer* (New York: Church Publishing, Inc., 1979), 308.
2. Dmitry in *The Brothers Karamazov* by Fyodor Dostoevsky. Cited in Evgueny Lampert, *The Divine Realm* (London: Faber & Faber, 1944), 104–5.
3. Kurt Weitzmann, et al., *The Icon* (New York: Alfred A. Knopf, 1982), 4.
4. From the CD *Church of the Advocate Presents Peace of the Road*; liner notes from the CD.
5. Meredith Monk in *Crossroads: Art and Religion in American Life*, ed. Alberta Arthurs and Glenn Wallach (New York: The New Press, 2001), 251.

Conclusion

Pilgrimage Congregations

Diana Butler Bass
Virginia Theological Seminary
Alexandria, Virginia

Upon first reading the essays that make up this book, we experienced the surprise of Graham Standish's "divine coincidences." Although the pastors sharing these stories had never met, we noticed that certain common themes were threaded throughout their accounts of congregational change. In every case, leaders practiced discernment by paying attention to cultural change, listening to the voices of the congregation, and relating the biblical story and God's call to the gathered community. The practice of hospitality looms large in the narratives as congregations pondered the question of how to welcome an array of strangers in their midst. In addition, emotive and participatory worship practices emerge as key to vital faith communities.[1] The triad of those practices—discernment, hospitality, and worship—laid the foundation of congregational spiritual depth and vitality. Throughout the essays, we heard what we as researchers had already witnessed in our study: intentional engagement with Christian tradition as embodied in faith practices fostered a renewed sense of identity and mission in congregations. At first, we called such churches "practicing congregations," but increasingly, we have come to think of them as "pilgrimage congregations," communities of Christian practice moving toward the ultimate goal of knowing God.

Part of our concern about the term "practicing congregations" arose from the temptation to think of Christian practice as a new program of congregational renewal—a kind of mainline Protestant "forty days of purpose" marketing scheme. For the pilgrim congregations we met in our research, renewal based only in numerical growth—in terms of fixing the building, adding to the membership rolls, or proselytizing—was not the primary goal. Rather, in every case, the pastor and people sought to create or renew a congregation that would touch the lives of spiritual nomads—serving as spiritual bridges from the nomadic life to a life of faithful discipleship. The congregations whose stories are told here resist the urge toward becoming a program of church growth. Rather, they represent an encouraging possibility of Christian communal life, that of the organic body of Christ journeying toward shalom, as a realistic and hopeful model for other congregations.

In some cases the nomads had been members of the church, people longing for a deeper experience of the Christian life; in other cases nomads were strangers—children, the unchurched, gay and lesbian members, the homeless, artists, or social justice activists—seeking to connect with God. Discernment helped the congregation see the stranger; hospitality welcomed the stranger; and worship provided strangers a connection to the community and to God. Working together, these three practices not only opened the way to congregational renewal, but they initiated the movement of the individual from being a spiritual tourist to being a Christian pilgrim. The renewed congregation served as the locus for personal transformation. Pilgrimage congregations birth Christian pilgrims.

What was also obvious, however, was that despite their commonalities, the congregations were distinct communities of faith. No two followed the same path to vitality. Each church is a unique local adaptation of the Christian tradition. The core of discernment, hospitality, and worship had pointed them toward other specific practices to which God uniquely called their community—things like sharing testimonies, saying yes and saying no, taking risks, sharing the Word, engaging in the arts, and practicing contemplation. These distinctive practices give, to use Steve Jacobsen's image, the garden character, reflecting the "local ecosystem" of God's grace. Thus, we learned that locality played a large role in determining the specific forms of Christian tradition and practice that emerged in each congregation.

Beyond the creative persistence of locality, however, we could discern some larger cultural patterns in the congregations. Despite the distinct ways in which these congregations address local situations, particular traits of American postmodern culture appear in all these stories. In different ways and different places, they refracted the stresses of contemporary individualism, aimlessness, consumption, fragmentation, and forgetfulness—the conditions of American life that foster nomadic spirituality. To overcome the fracturing of postmodern life, they reached backward toward the historic Great Tradition, that which Huston Smith calls "the voice of peace, justice and beauty that emanated from the Christian soul."[2] By reaching back and drawing out wisdom for today, they responded (sometimes overtly, sometimes intuitively) to these five postmodern traits, in effect inverting a potentially destructive cultural pattern into a faith-filled way of life. By providing intentional congregations based on Christian practice, they offered a path for nomads to become pilgrims.

Individualism:
From Nomads to Pilgrims

Cultural theorists note that one of the dominating characteristics of postmodern life is that of wandering—moving from experience to experience for the sake of experience alone. Of necessity, wandering is an individualistic activity, with occasional "joining," "meeting up," "networking," or "hooking up" with other individual wanderers for a limited period and for a particular experience. Radical practices of individual autonomy mark contemporary spirituality, with each person serving as arbiter of personal ethics, moral choice, and religious preference. As two British scholars explain, "The goal is not to defer to higher authority, but to have the courage to become one's own authority. Not to follow established path, but to forge one's own inner-directed, as subjective, life."[3]

From "Sheila-ism" in *Habits of the Heart* to a recent *Newsweek/Beliefnet* poll in which 24 percent of Americans claim to be "spiritual but not religious," the turn toward spiritual individualism is well documented.[4] Indeed, philosopher Charles Taylor claims that all contemporary changes can be related to a single process, "the massive subjective turn of modern culture."[5]

Such trends trouble many mainline pastors and church leaders. After all, traditional religions, like mainline Protestantism, are organized communally—usually along lines of family, class, and inherited customs and traditions. Indeed, recent studies suggest that increased spiritual autonomy directly—and negatively—affects mainstream religions. How can traditional churches survive in a "spiritual but not religious" culture?

In our research we found that congregations able to link the longings for spiritual experience with the Christian tradition not only survived, but they appeared to be thriving. Indeed, instead of condemning or fearing individual spiritual autonomy, they welcomed it as a precondition for renewed Christian faith.[6] Perhaps the clearest example in these stories is that of Phinney Ridge Lutheran Church in Seattle. In a city where more than 80 percent of people do not attend church, Phinney Ridge invites spiritual wanderers into a life of worship, study, prayer, and service. At Phinney Ridge, they recognize that individual longing acts as the entryway to a deeper life of faith. Over a fourteen-year period, making nomads into pilgrims has been the congregation's primary vocation—and it has transformed hundreds of individuals and their church.

Aimlessness:
From Busyness to Vocation

Postmodern people possess no stable identity, nothing is inherited from the past, no family ties bind, and all forms of personhood must be chosen and, often, chosen again. It is not uncommon for an individual to live in several states, marry more than once, change religious traditions one or more times, and switch jobs or entire careers. Indeed, the impulse toward instability is so pronounced that some postmodern theorists believe that constant questing for personal meaning (and never finding any) is the only sane way to adapt to contemporary life. Life is an unfinished and unfinishable project. Much of postmodernism suggests that meaninglessness is life's ultimate meaning. Human beings are, in essence, homeless wanderers. And this wandering, the constant roaming for identity, fuels random busyness—often as a way to cover the sense that everything may well be meaningless.

As a counterpoint to postmodern homelessness, Christian pilgrims have a dynamic role and ultimate destination. Pilgrims find identity in baptism, the sacrament that knits them into the body of Christ and defines the self in relation to God's story and the story of God's people. Baptism also calls pilgrims to other practices—things like hospitality, peacemaking, justice, and charity—that deepen a sense of Christian identity.

In his essay, Steve Jacobsen shares how an eclectic group of questing individuals can ground themselves, through the very diversity of their wanderings, in Christian tradition. At Goleta Presbyterian, a variety of meanings, perspectives, and experiences serve to break up the hard soil of "monocultural" Christian identity, allowing for the possibility that postmodern searching can actually be the mealy soil of pilgrimage. Goleta regularly witnesses "nomads" who stay. "They exchange their nomad identities (wanderers without a home)," writes Steve, "for pilgrim identities (people on a journey who believe they have a home)." He continues, "That 'home' is a reverence for God founding the practice of reverence for one another, as exemplified in Jesus' ministry." And, although they find "home," that "home" is not a fixed place or predetermined identity. It remains a continual quest, but now a Christian quest, for meaning and authenticity through Jesus Christ and the community of the church.

One of the strongest senses of finding home comes through the vocation of worship, of inviting wanderers into the work of God's people in liturgy. In Gary Jones's essay about Holy Communion and Eric Elnes's story of Scottsdale Congregational, worship is not simply liturgical busywork or some sort of Christian entertainment geared to fill an hour on Sunday morning. In each case, even with their very different approaches, worship opens the congregation to a sense of God's presence, "a holy place," to quote theologian Thomas Kelly, "to which we may continuously return." Each pastor reflects on the quality of homecoming in worship, of discovering oneself in God's story, and of "reframing life." Worship leads the way home.

In our study, it intrigued us to see how many of the congregations had ministries serving the homeless. Many people mentioned how, despite the fact that they live in houses, that they, too, "felt homeless" and experienced a surprising kinship to the actual homeless people they befriended. Because of their sense of dislocation, many expressed that homeless people had taught them about the spiritual life, trust, stewardship, healing, and commitment. Throughout the research, we regularly heard mainline churchgoers refer to themselves as wayfarers, sojourners, and pilgrims—all images that conjure a sense of spatial dislocation and spiritual relocation in God. Their renewed sense of identity gave them a new sense of vocation—faithfully living out the practices that compose a Christian way of life.

Consumption:
From Consumers to Practitioners

Across the globe, people participate in postmodern culture primarily through what they buy or aspire to buy. As one Church of England report puts it, "Where previous generations found their identity in what they produced, we now find our identity in what we consume."[7] Christians have not escaped the pervasive consumerism that defines religious identities, traditions, and faith practices. Indeed, postmodern consumer culture is so powerful that it absorbs "all other cultures as 'content' to be commodified, distributed, and consumed," in a way that renders faith increasingly unable to reshape our lives.[8] In the process, Christian symbols and practices themselves often become products in service to consumerism, a faith that can be marketed to spiritual nomads.

Several of the stories offered here directly challenge consumerist Christianity. Instead of just buying the latest technological thing for worship, the people of Goleta Presbyterian have learned to use new technologies intentionally in relation to their congregational life. At All Souls Cathedral in Asheville, North Carolina, the congregation has resisted the temptation to turn the arts into a spiritual commodity. Rather than making beauty the purview of the wealthy, All Souls has created practices of radical hospitality around the arts—opening visual arts and music to the whole community regardless of social status or income. In two Methodist churches in North Carolina, minister Ken Carter helped his congregations navigate the mass-culture phenomena of *The Prayer of Jabez* and *The Passion of the Christ.* In all these cases, congregations engaged in Christian practices (silence, sabbatical, hospitality, and saying yes and saying no) as correctives to consumer culture—thus guiding members further into a life of reflective pilgrimage.

Fragmentation: From Individuals to Gathered Community

Personal autonomy, subjectively driven lives, and consumer choice lead in a predictable direction: toward cultural fragmentation. After all, individuals come to separate and distinct understandings of meaning, with people appealing to a variety of moral, ethical, and spiritual authorities for guidance. Although large numbers of people still choose to assent to certain loci of authority (such as the U.S. Constitution or the Roman Catholic Church), the possibility for interpreting even traditional authorities is nearly endless. In his recent book, *The World Is Flat,* Thomas Friedman points out that top-down, centralized, chain-of-command authorities are quickly becoming history as networks of participatory and relational authorities take their place.[9] The shift from established authorities to emerging ones is a process of chaotic cultural reorganization whereby fragmentation is an inevitable part of the journey of change.

In an age of fragmentation, however, many people are tempted to revert back to top-down authority as a way of controlling chaos. All of the churches in our study are part of denominations where some interest groups are attempting to centralize doctrine, polity, and praxis as an answer to fractured culture. Throughout our research, however, we observed that these congregations moved in the exact opposite way—away from being hierarchical, top-down communities of authority toward more participatory forms of church. Instead of reasserting the ministerial or doctrinal voice of authority, they opened their congregations to more voices, bringing a multiplicity of perspectives to bear on community life. As a result of embracing variety, the worshiping assembly generated spiritual authority—shifting Christian leadership away from external and distant sources to the inner work of paying attention to the Holy Spirit. By moving more deeply into diversity, they formed the New Testament vision of church being Christ's body in the world.

In these essays, Church of the Redeemer in New Haven exemplifies this finding. The practice of testimony shifts religious authority away from the minister toward the gathered congregation—moral example, religious instruction, done by the community and through the community's experience of God in its midst. Perhaps the most striking line in pastor Lillian Daniel's essay is, "My sermon that day was on spiritual practices, but I could have thrown it out and no one would have noticed." Testimony led Redeemer away from the old minister-centered model of civic leadership into a new expression of the ancient tradition of New England democratic faith. The congregation learned the power of sharing the Word in community—and how a community is created through hospitality, Sabbath keeping, and healing.

Another, and perhaps more surprising, story of the shift from fragmentation to participatory community comes from St. Philip's Episcopal Church in Durham, North Carolina. Given their denomination's hierarchical structure, it would be historically easy for Episcopal parishes to lean on top-down solutions to contemporary problems. During a time of stressful denominational divides over homosexuality, the Reverend Scott Benhase offers a hopeful story about one congregation's ability to overcome factions by creating a community of discernment, trust, and love. By sharing leadership, they were able to take risks that threaten to destroy other congregations.

Forgetfulness:
From Amnesia to Memory

The final quality of contemporary life that sustains nomadic spirituality is forgetfulness. Mobility, technology, education, changes in women's roles, divorce, cohabitation, travel, and urbanization all combine to cut people off from sources of memory—family, neighborhood, and heritage. In a fragmented and decentralized culture, it is easy to forget (and sometimes purposely so) the chain of memory that ties past, present, and future. Forgetfulness has deep consequences for religious communities. French theorist Danielle Hervieu-Léger goes so far as to argue that contemporary societies are less religious because they are "less and less capable of maintaining the memory which lies at the heart of religious existence." They have become "amnesic societies."[10]

First Church, Cambridge, Massachusetts, was founded in 1636 and is one of the oldest churches in the United States—not the kind of congregation likely to forget its past. Yet, as pastor Mary Luti relates, it was in danger of forgetting its children. By forgetting them, the congregation discovered that it was endangering the whole process of Christian memory. In remembering the children, however, they learned that their "common life" centered "decisively" on the ancient practice of hospitality—thus reshaping the whole congregation as a way of life that welcomes all to God.

In all the essays shared, pastors tell stories of memory—times when their congregations reached back to recover lost traditions of the biblical story, worship, prayer, justice, and formation. In an age of forgetfulness, these are communities of memory—not of stilted traditions, but living ones that connect people to the past. Through remembering, spiritual nomads locate themselves in a story, finding new traditions, a "goodly heritage," and a new family. By remembering identity, wanderers can find a home with Christian pilgrims. They are still seeking God, but remembering shapes the journey's direction and purpose.

How to turn tourists into pilgrims? The stories we have heard and shared offer a compelling vision of church as pilgrimage communities, communities of practice that invert the characteristics of chaos into marks of Christian discipleship. We noticed that, unlike fundamentalist Christians, the mainline congregations involved in our research did not spurn the surrounding culture. Rather, they used the longings, fears, and aspirations of contemporary experience as entry points to a Christian way of life. They manage to speak to the unique historical moment with a faithful voice. And they taught us that it is virtually impossible to make the leap from nomad to pilgrim without a community, without friends on the journey.

As Roy Terry explained so well of his congregation, Cornerstone United Methodist, they are all "becoming church" by reconnecting with the biblical story, Christian tradition, and faith practices in a journey of authentic community. In every case, these communities opened their hearts to the Spirit and their minds to creative imagination. No two congregations we studied were alike, but as these essays reveal, their collective experiences form a stained-glass window of change. The pieces, colors, and patterns fit together in surprising ways. The windows tell a story. Stand back and look. You will see pilgrims on a journey. And you may well see the prisms of a new kind of Christianity being born.

Notes

1. By "emotive," we do not mean "emotional." Rather, "emotive" is intended to convey worship that engages the whole person—mind, spirit, emotions, and body—through a surprisingly wide variety of liturgical and musical styles.

2. Huston Smith, *The Soul of Christianity: Restoring the Great Tradition* (San Francisco: HarperSanFrancisco, 2005), vii.

3. Paul Heelas, Linda Woodhead, et al., *The Spiritual Revolution: Why Religion Is Giving Way to Spirituality* (London: Blackwell, 2005), 4.

4. Robert Bellah et al., *Habits of the Heart: Individualism and Commitment in American Life* (Berkeley: Univ. of California Press, 1985), remains the seminal book in understanding the growth of religious individualism. The poll is found in *Newsweek*, "In Search of the Spiritual" (September 5, 2005), 48–49. For a recent and challenging study on "spiritual but not religious," see Heelas and Woodhead, *The Spiritual Revolution*.

5. Quoted in Heelas and Woodhead, *The Spiritual Revolution*, 2.

6. In his book *Spiritual Marketplace* (Berkeley: Univ. of California Press, 1999), Wade Clark Roof suggests that "Sheila-ism" might be "spiritual rejuvenating" as a "means of positive self-assertion and inner discovery" (p. 149). Interestingly enough, the *Newsweek*/Beliefnet poll states that 55 percent of Americans self-identify as "religious and spiritual," suggestive that Roof's assertion that "Sheila-ism" could be a resource for religious congregations. But the *Newsweek* statistic was left unexplained—with no indication of how or where Americans were putting together the impulses of personal spirituality and religious tradition. Our research suggests that, at least in some instances, Roof may well be right, and Americans are doing so in congregations like the ones we describe in *The Practicing Congregation: Imagining a New Old Church* (Herndon, VA: Alban, 2004), and in *From Nomads to Pilgrims.*

7. *Mission-Shaped Church: Church Planting and Fresh Expressions of Church in a Changing Context* (London: Church House Publishing, 2004), 9.

8. Vincent J. Miller, *Consuming Religion: Christian Faith and Practice in a Consumer Culture* (New York: Continuum, 2004), 179.

9. Thomas L. Friedman, *The World Is Flat: A Brief History of the Twenty-First Century* (New York: Farrar, Straus, and Giroux, 2005). See also Manuel Castells, *The Rise of the Network Society*, 2nd ed. (London: Blackwell, 2000).
10. Danielle Hervieu-Léger, *Religion as a Chain of Memory*, Eng. ed. (New Brunswick, NJ: Rutgers, 2000).

ABOUT THE PROJECT

The Project on Congregations of Intentional Practice was a three-year study of vital mainline congregations conducted from 2002 through 2005 by Diana Butler Bass, Ph.D., and Joseph Stewart-Sicking, Ed.D. It was funded by Lilly Endowment Inc., and housed at the Virginia Theological Seminary in Alexandria, Virginia. The project has also published Diana Butler Bass, *The Practicing Congregation: Imagining a New Old Church* (Alban, 2004). In the fall of 2006 the final book related to the project will be released: Diana Butler Bass, *Christianity for the Rest of Us* (HarperSanFrancisco). For contact information, research details, news, project events, and updates, see www.practicingcongregations.org.